the THESAURUS *for* KIDS

By Evelyn Pesiri
Illustrated by Linda Bild

To Elizabeth Ross, friend indeed
— E. P.

Created by: RGA Publishing Group, Inc., Lisa Melton, Editor-in-Chief

Designed by: Brenda Leach

Computer imaging by: The Hi-Rez Studio™

Cover photo by: Ann Bogart

Published by McClanahan Book Company, Inc.
23 West 26th Street, New York, NY 10010
Printed in the U.S.A.
ISBN 1-56293-355-8

Writing with Flying Colors
(or, How to Use a Thesaurus to Improve Your Writing)

Do you sometimes have  butterflies in your stomach about writing?

Is expanding your vocabulary  an uphill climb?

Well, you don't have to  bend over backward anymore to find just the right word for your writing, because *The Thesaurus for Kids* is here.

What exactly *is* a thesaurus? First and foremost, it's a powerful tool to help you make your writing lively and interesting. That includes the reports and essays you write for school, as well as the stories, poems, and anything else you might write for yourself. A thesaurus is also a great way to expand your speaking and reading vocabularies, and when that happens, your writing will automatically improve.

Like a dictionary, a thesaurus is a list of words in alphabetical order. Each word is called an *entry word.* But while a dictionary tells you the meaning (or meanings) of each entry word, a thesaurus gives you a list of *synonyms*. Synonyms are close in meaning to the entry word, and they are the reason for using a thesaurus in the first place—to find an alternate word for something you want to write or say.

When to Use a Thesaurus

Just as a soccer coach might send in a substitute player to make a game better, you might "send in" substitute words to make your writing better. That's when you should reach for *The Thesaurus for Kids*. For example, let's say you write the following sentence:

The children climbed to the top of the cliff.

Does it sound too ordinary to you? Or perhaps too boring? Well, spice it up! Use your thesaurus and look up the entry word **cliff**. Look over the synonyms, then send in the substitute player!

The children climbed to the top of the *precipice*.

What if you want to improve your sentence further? Look up **climb**.

The children *clambered* to the top of the *precipice*.

Now you know how to put the thesaurus to work for you. You chose more interesting words. Now check to see that your new sentence fits what you want to say.

Choosing the *Right* Synonym

In each entry, the synonyms differ in some way. One synonym may be closer in meaning to the entry word than another. One may be more intense—for example, **famished** means not just "hungry," but "very hungry." Now compare the words **smart** and **ingenious**. Although this thesaurus lists *ingenious* as a synonym for *smart,* most people would agree that an ingenious idea is even smarter than a smart idea. So choose the synonym that best matches the idea you want to communicate! Just how smart is the idea? *You* are the writer—*you* decide!

Try to avoid words that are overused, such as **good** or **big** or **look**. Replace these words with more colorful synonyms, such as **admirable** or **massive** or **glance**. As you write a story or report, also consider *who will* *read it.* For instance, if a story is for your little brother, using the word **pallid** to replace the word **pale** might not be a good idea, but your teacher might like it!

Remember that in choosing the right synonym, you must be careful! Some synonyms are used only in certain contexts. For example, the word **vacant** is shown as a synonym for the entry word **empty**. While **vacant** can be used to describe an empty house, it can't be used to describe an empty glass. The sample phrases provided for many of the entry words will help you determine how a certain synonym may be used.

Special Features of Your Thesaurus

Your thesaurus doesn't stop at providing lists of synonyms for entry words. It also has other special features. These features are summarized in the legend box located on most right-hand pages of the book. Here's what the legend looks like:

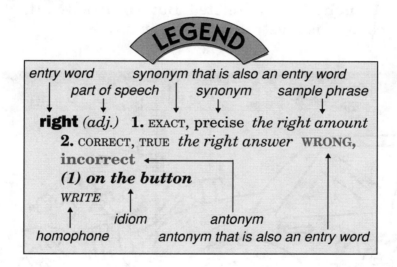

entry word: shown in **boldface** type. When an entry word is listed more than once, it's being used for different parts of speech.

part of speech: shown in *italic.*

synonym: a word close in meaning to the entry word. *When a synonym is* CAPITALIZED, *it can be looked up as an entry word.*

sample phrase: shown in *italic.* When an entry word has more than one meaning, the meanings are numbered and a sample phrase is given for each meaning. The sample phrase shows how the entry word might be used in a phrase or sentence.

antonym: shown in blue type. An antonym is a word opposite in meaning to the entry word.
When an antonym is CAPITALIZED, *it can be looked up as an entry word.*

idiom: shown in ***bold italic.*** An idiom is a colorful phrase whose meaning does not come from the individual words that make it up. Rather, its meaning is close to that of the entry word. When an entry word has more than one meaning, the idiom is numbered to correspond with the set of synonyms to which it belongs.

homophone: shown in *CAPITALIZED ITALIC.* A homophone is pronounced the same as the entry word but is spelled differently and has a different meaning.

The Thesaurus for Kids also includes two additional features. In one, you get to **Guess the Idiom** that goes with a humorous illustration. The entry word provides a clue. **Go Crazy with Words** shows you illustrated clusters of words that are related in meaning. For instance, **damp**, **wet**, **soaked**, and **drenched** are all related. But which do you think is wetter, damp or drenched? The illustration gives you a clue.

Going on a Word Search

Remember that in searching for the right synonym, only you know what word you want. If you do not find the perfect synonym the first place you look, don't give up. Instead, go on a word search!

A word search works something like this: Say you are writing a story about a big monster. Using your thesaurus, you turn to the entry word **big** to find the perfect synonym. But you do not find one that you like. You see that the synonym **HUGE** is shown in capital letters. Turn to the page where **huge** is included as an entry word. You might find the perfect word there! (How about **colossal**?) If you don't find the word, don't stop your search. Continue until you've found exactly the right word you need to express your thoughts.

A Final Word

Remember that to a writer, there's no better friend than a thesaurus.

And using one is  a piece of cake!

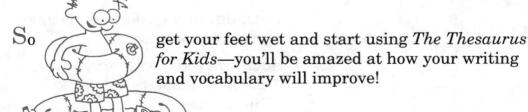

So get your feet wet and start using *The Thesaurus for Kids*—you'll be amazed at how your writing and vocabulary will improve!

Aa

• •

abandon *(v.)* **1.** DESERT, forsake, SURRENDER, LEAVE, strand, cede *abandon the ship* **recover** **2.** withdraw, RECALL *abandon the argument*

ability *(n.)* **1.** SKILL, TALENT, dexterity, knack, GIFT, aptitude *She had great athletic ability.* **inability** **2.** means, POWER, capacity *the ability to pay* **inability**

able *(adj.)* FIT, talented, skillful, capable, QUALIFIED, practiced, apt, competent, proficient, adept, deft **unable, incompetent** *on the ball*

◆ **Guess the Idiom** ◆

clue: able

• •

answer: on the ball

---

about *(prep.)* **1.** concerning, regarding *a book about animals* **2.** ALMOST, nearly, around, approximately *about five dollars* **exactly, precisely**

above *(adv.)* over, aloft, beyond **below**

absent *(adj.)* missing, away, lacking **PRESENT**

absorb *(v.)* **1.** sop, sponge, consume, swallow *absorb the water with a sponge* **2.** cushion *absorb the shock*

absurd *(adj.)* FOOLISH, SILLY, RIDICULOUS, STUPID, idiotic, asinine, inane **rational, reasonable, sensible**

abuse *(n.)* misuse, mistreatment, deception, injury

abuse *(v.)* HURT, INJURE, misuse, mistreat, violate, defile *walk all over*

accept *(v.)* **1.** BELIEVE, TRUST, APPROVE, ADMIT, endure *accept the excuse* **mistrust** **2.** TAKE, RECEIVE *accept the invitation* **REFUSE, decline** **3.** ASSUME, undertake *accept the responsibility* **DENY**

accident *(n.)* misfortune, mishap, DISASTER, casualty

accurate *(adj.)* CORRECT, EXACT, precise, sound **INACCURATE, imprecise**

accuse *(v.)* BLAME, CHARGE, denounce

ache *(v.)* HURT, throb

achieve *(v.)* accomplish, REACH, COMPLETE, DO, FULFILL **FAIL**

acquire *(v.)* OBTAIN, GET, GAIN **LOSE**

act *(n.)* deed, feat, achievement, performance, exploit

act *(v.)* behave, WORK, PERFORM, OPERATE, execute

action *(n.)* movement, gesture, deed, feat, performance

active *(adj.)* **1.** BUSY, ENERGETIC, dynamic, LIVELY, frisky, vigorous *an active puppy* IDLE, LAZY, inactive **2.** ALERT *an active mind* IDLE, inactive

activity *(n.)* ACTION, TASK, chore, WORK, LABOR, undertaking, venture

actual *(adj.)* **1.** TRUE, GENUINE, CERTAIN *an actual flag from the Civil War* imitation, FAKE **2.** REAL, tangible, concrete, material *What's the actual cost of the computer?* IMAGINARY

adapt *(v.)* ADJUST, FIT, SUIT, modify, conform

add *(v.)* **1.** sum up, TOTAL *Add the numbers to get the answer.* SUBTRACT **2.** EXTEND, INCREASE, JOIN, unite, supplement, ENLARGE *We plan to add a room to the house.* DECREASE, REMOVE **3.** complement *The hat adds to the outfit.* detract

adequate *(adj.)* ENOUGH, sufficient, ample, SATISFACTORY inadequate, lacking

adjust *(v.)* CHANGE, modify, regulate, SET, alter

admire *(v.)* appreciate, CHERISH, RESPECT, regard, esteem, venerate

admit *(v.)* **1.** CONFESS, own up, concede, acknowledge, avow *Admit the truth.* DENY **2.** let in, PERMIT, ACCEPT *Admit the visitor.*

adore *(v.)* ADMIRE, LOVE, HONOR, WORSHIP, revere, idolize, venerate HATE, DESPISE, loathe

adorn *(v.)* DECORATE, beautify, enrich, grace

advance *(v.)* **1.** APPROACH, proceed *Advance toward the finish line.* withdraw, retreat **2.** progress, further, BETTER, RISE, thrive, IMPROVE, flourish *Advance within the company.*

adventure *(n.)* EXPERIENCE, exploit, undertaking

advice *(n.)* guidance, counsel, tip, pointer

affect *(v.)* **1.** INFLUENCE, alter, CHANGE, sway, CONCERN, modify *His injury will affect the outcome of the game.* **2.** impress, touch, STIR *The teacher's lectures affect everyone.*

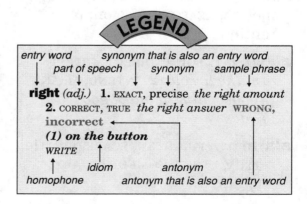

LEGEND

entry word   synonym that is also an entry word
part of speech   synonym   sample phrase

right *(adj.)* **1.** EXACT, precise *the right amount* **2.** CORRECT, TRUE *the right answer* WRONG, incorrect
(1) on the button
WRITE

homophone   idiom   antonym
antonym that is also an entry word

afraid (adj.) frightened, scared, fearful, terrified, TIMID, alarmed FEARLESS, **unafraid,** DARING, BOLD, CONFIDENT

after (prep.) afterward, following, later, subsequently, behind, next BEFORE

aggravate (v.) **1.** IRRITATE, ANNOY, exasperate *He aggravates me.* **2.** intensify, EXAGGERATE, worsen, exacerbate *Don't aggravate the problem.*
(2) rock the boat, add fuel to the fire

agony (n.) **1.** PAIN, torment, torture, suffering, distress, pang *the agony of a broken leg* **2.** anguish, misery, heartache, woe *the agony of defeat*

agree (v.) concur, CONFIRM, consent, YIELD, APPROVE, PERMIT, SUPPORT, assent DISAGREE, **differ, oppose**

aid (n.) HELP, assistance, benefit, RELIEF, service.

aid (v.) HELP, ASSIST, SUPPORT, relieve, BACK **hinder, deter**

aim (n.) GOAL, PURPOSE, objective, motive, REASON, mission, intention

aim (v.) **1.** POINT, DIRECT, target *aim the arrow* **2.** INTEND, MEAN, propose *aim to make good grades*

alarm (v.) FRIGHTEN, SCARE, startle, terrify, UPSET COMFORT, CALM, SOOTHE

alert (v.) WARN, CAUTION, INFORM, SIGNAL

alert (adj.) **1.** attentive, vigilant, AWARE, wary, watchful *The students were alert this morning.* inattentive **2.** LIVELY, spry, QUICK, INTELLIGENT *a very alert newborn colt* DULL
(1) on your toes

alike (adj.) similar, SAME, like, IDENTICAL, twin, matching DIFFERENT

allow (v.) LET, PERMIT, consent, grant, APPROVE, LICENSE **prohibit,** FORBID, **inhibit**
give the green light

almost (adv.) nearly, somewhat, approximately, around, ABOUT, roughly

alone (adj.) solitary, apart, isolated, LONELY, lone, SINGLE, PRIVATE **accompanied**
out in the cold

◆ **Guess the Idiom** ◆

clue: alone

answer: out in the cold

always *(adv.)* forever, eternally, perpetually, evermore, forevermore NEVER

amaze *(v.)* SURPRISE, THRILL, FASCINATE, stun, bewilder, ASTONISH, astound, captivate **bore**

amount *(n.)* NUMBER, QUANTITY, score, tally, TOTAL, sum, bulk, capacity, volume

amuse *(v.)* PLEASE, TICKLE, DELIGHT, ENTERTAIN **displease**

ancient *(adj.)* OLD, aged, antique MODERN, NEW

anger *(n.)* RAGE, fury, wrath, ire

anger *(v.)* AGGRAVATE, IRRITATE, madden, ANNOY
make one's blood boil

angry *(adj.)* annoyed, IRRITABLE, resentful, stormy, furious, infuriated, enraged, raging, antagonistic, indignant, irate, wrathful, livid **pleased, gratified**
hot under the collar

announce *(v.)* DECLARE, proclaim

annoy *(v.)* DISTURB, nag, pester, BOTHER, displease, TROUBLE, IRRITATE, OFFEND, AGGRAVATE, provoke, exasperate, plague PLEASE, **gratify, appease**
get on someone's nerves

annoyed *(adj.)* irritated, bothered, upset, ANGRY, FURIOUS, livid **pleased, gratified, satisfied**

answer *(n.)* response, REPLY, explanation, solution, reaction, retort QUESTION, **query**

Go CRAZY with WORDS!

annoyed

11

answer *(v.)* RESPOND, REPLY, EXPLAIN, SOLVE, react, retort ASK, QUESTION, **query**

anxious *(adj.)* NERVOUS, worried, RESTLESS, concerned, disturbed, uneasy, apprehensive **relaxed, CALM**
having butterflies in one's stomach

◆ **Guess the Idiom** ◆

clue: anxious

answer: having butterflies in one's stomach

apologize *(v.)* REGRET, DEFEND, allege, ANSWER

appear *(v.)* **1.** COME, ARRIVE, arise, surface, emerge, SHOW *appear at noon* VANISH, DISAPPEAR **2.** SEEM, LOOK *The answer may appear correct.*

appearance *(n.)* **1.** LOOK *She has a nice appearance.* **2.** guise, semblance, pretext *Although quite interested, he had a deliberately bored appearance.*

appetite *(n.)* hunger, craving, DESIRE, longing, thirst, lust, demand

applaud *(v.)* CHEER, PRAISE, CLAP, APPROVE BOO, **disapprove, hiss**

appreciate *(v.)* **1.** prize, value, treasure, relish *appreciate one's parents* **2.** UNDERSTAND, comprehend, acknowledge *appreciate one's point of view*

approach *(v.)* **1.** ADVANCE, NEAR, APPROXIMATE, impend, converge *Approach the injured dog with caution.* **2.** address, propose, INTRODUCE *waiting for a good time to approach the subject*

appropriate *(adj.)* FIT, suitable, relevant, pertinent **unfit, unsuitable, irrelevant**

approve *(v.)* APPLAUD, commend, attest, endorse, ratify DISAPPROVE, **dispute**

approximate *(v.)* **1.** ADVANCE, NEAR *Approximate the starting line.* **2.** ESTIMATE, appraise, compute, figure *Approximate the answer.*

approximate *(adj.)* NEAR, rough, inexact, CLOSE, imprecise

area *(n.)* **1.** SPACE, REGION, territory, district, quarter *We live in the area.* **2.** department, field, sphere *Modern art is her area of interest.*

argue *(v.)* DISAGREE, QUARREL, quibble, FIGHT, differ, haggle, DEBATE, dispute AGREE *lock horns*

• Guess the Idiom •

clue: argue

....

answer: lock horns

arrange *(v.)* ORGANIZE, ORDER, PLACE **disarrange**

arrest *(v.)* **1.** CAPTURE, CATCH, apprehend, detain, nab *Arrest the criminal.* **2.** STOP, STAY, CHECK, DELAY, BLOCK, retard, inhibit *By educating people, we hope to arrest the spread of disease.* **promote**

arrive *(v.)* COME, REACH, APPEAR **LEAVE, DEPART**

artificial *(adj.)* synthetic, unreal, unnatural, FALSE, counterfeit, FAKE **REAL, genuine**

ashamed *(adj.)* embarrassed, shamefaced, abashed **PROUD**

ask *(v.)* QUESTION, INQUIRE, query, REQUEST, appeal, interrogate, petition, entreat, solicit **RESPOND, ANSWER**

assemble *(v.)* **1.** GATHER, COLLECT, convene *The students assemble in the school auditorium.* SCATTER **2.** BUILD, erect, CONSTRUCT, fabricate, MANUFACTURE *Assemble the model car.* **disassemble**

assign *(v.)* appoint, allot, allocate

assist *(v.)* HELP, AID, SERVE, relieve, SUPPORT **hinder, impede**

assume *(v.)* **1.** BELIEVE, infer, suppose, presume, SUSPECT *Let's assume we will win the game.* **2.** adopt, undertake, shoulder, ACCEPT *He assumed a new position on the team.* REJECT, **REFUSE, decline**

assure *(v.)* **1.** PROMISE, PLEDGE, affirm, attest, guarantee, certify *Assure the safety of the crew.* **2.** ENCOURAGE, enthuse, hearten *Assure the worried child.*

astonish *(v.)* SURPRISE, astound, AMAZE, dazzle, awe, stupefy, SHOCK, overwhelm

attach *(v.)* JOIN, FASTEN, secure, FIX, adhere, affix **DETACH, SEPARATE**

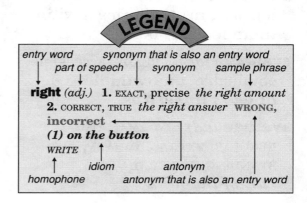

LEGEND

| entry word | | synonym that is also an entry word |
| part of speech | | synonym | sample phrase |

right *(adj.)* **1.** EXACT, precise *the right amount* **2.** CORRECT, TRUE *the right answer* **WRONG, incorrect**
(1) on the button
WRITE

homophone | idiom | antonym | antonym that is also an entry word

13

attack (*n.*) RAID, invasion, offense, onslaught **retreat**

attack (*v.*) RAID, CHARGE, INVADE, STORM, assault, encroach **retreat, DEFEND**

attempt (*v.*) TRY, undertake, STRUGGLE, strive, toil, AIM, endeavor, venture

attend (*v.*) **1.** VISIT, FREQUENT, haunt *Will you attend the party?* **2.** LISTEN, heed, harken *Attend the teacher.* IGNORE, **disregard 3.** nurse, AID, ASSIST *Attend the sick pony.* **4.** escort, chaperone, accompany, usher *Attend to the younger children on Halloween.*

attitude (*n.*) **1.** pose, posture, POSITION, bearing, deportment *The wrestler approached his opponent with an attitude of aggression.* **2.** disposition, presence, air, demeanor *She has a calm attitude.*

attract (*v.*) DRAW, PULL, TEMPT, LURE, COAX, BAIT, charm, allure, entice **repel** *catch someone's eye*

attractive (*adj.*) LOVELY, appealing, BEAUTIFUL, alluring, inviting **unappealing, UGLY**

available (*adj.*) READY, accessible, obtainable **unavailable** *at one's fingertips*

average (*adj.*) NORMAL, USUAL, REGULAR **EXTRAORDINARY, OUTSTANDING, UNUSUAL** *run-of-the-mill*

avoid (*v.*) DODGE, MISS, ESCAPE, shun, shirk, hedge, elude, evade SEEK

award (*n.*) REWARD, decoration, medal, trophy, medallion

aware (*adj.*) attentive, observant, watchful, ALERT, vigilant **unaware, unobservant**

awful (*adj.*) dreadful, appalling, frightful, HORRIBLE, shocking, disagreeable, objectionable **WONDERFUL, terrific, GREAT**

awkward (*adj.*) CLUMSY, cumbersome, inept **agile, dexterous** *all thumbs*

Bb

baby (*n.*) newborn, infant, tot, toddler

back (*n.*) REAR, posterior **FRONT, anterior**

bad (*adj.*) **1.** NAUGHTY, mischievous, DISHONEST, spoiled, WICKED, EVIL, shady, unfit, IMMORAL, CORRUPT, sinful *a bad character* GOOD **2.** ROTTEN, spoiled *bad meat* FRESH **3.** faulty, defective, dysfunctional, impaired *a bad battery*

baffle (*v.*) PUZZLE, bewilder, CONFUSE, mystify, perplex **enlighten, demystify**

bag (*n.*) sack, pouch

bait *(v.)* ATTRACT, LURE, snare, entice, entrap

ball *(n.)* **1.** globe, sphere, orb *Catch the ball.* **2.** DANCE, prom, masquerade, reception *Attend the ball.*
BAWL

ban *(v.)* FORBID, prohibit, outlaw, disallow, BAR, EXCLUDE, PREVENT **ALLOW, PERMIT**

band *(n.)* **1.** GROUP, GANG *band of musicians* **2.** STRIP, stripe, ribbon, belt *He wore a band around his waist.*

bar *(v.)* STOP, PREVENT, BLOCK, FORBID, EXCLUDE, barricade **ALLOW, PERMIT**

bare *(adj.)* **1.** naked, nude, un-clothed *a bare body* **CLOTHED** **2.** EMPTY, PLAIN, barren *a bare landscape* **lush**
BEAR

bargain *(n.)* **1.** DEAL, buy *Her new shirt was a bargain.* **2.** agreement, CONTRACT, transaction *I have a bargain with my father to make the team.*
(1) a steal

base *(n.)* **1.** BOTTOM, STAND, foundation *the base of the statue* **2.** ROOT, CAUSE, origin *the base of the problem*

basic *(adj.)* ESSENTIAL, fundamental, elementary, primary, rudimentary, SIMPLE

beach *(n.)* shore, seaside, COAST
BEECH

bear *(v.)* **1.** CARRY, TRANSPORT, CONVEY *Bear the flag.* **2.** STAND, suffer, tolerate, endure *Try to bear the pain.* **3.** PRODUCE, YIELD, REPRODUCE, beget, render, pro-create, propagate *bear young*
BARE

beat *(n.)* **1.** throb, pulse, pound *the beat of one's heart* **2.** tempo, meter, time, measure *the beat of the music*
BEET

beat *(v.)* **1.** WIN, DEFEAT, overcome, OVERTHROW, CONQUER, vanquish, thwart, surpass, SUCCEED, EXCEED, excel *Beat the team.* LOSE **2.** thrash, WHIP, lash, flog, maul, scourge *In Oliver Twist, the orphanage owner beats young Oliver.*
BEET

beautiful *(adj.)* PRETTY, LOVELY, ATTRACTIVE, FAIR, GORGEOUS, ravishing UGLY
a real knockout

beauty *(n.)* splendor, elegance, loveliness **ugliness**

become *(v.)* GROW, CHANGE, ADAPT

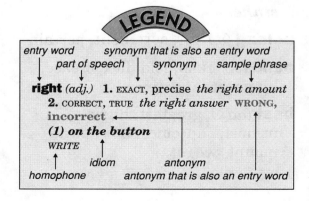

bed (*n.*) **1.** crib, bunk, berth, cot *sleep in a bed* **2.** patch, garden *plant strawberries in a bed*

before (*adv.*) prior, preceding, previously, earlier AFTER

beg (*v.*) plead, appeal, implore, entreat, beseech, petition, solicit, grovel,

begin (*v.*) START, commence, initiate, OPEN, INTRODUCE, launch, originate, arise END **get the ball rolling, get the show on the road**

beginner (*n.*) trainee, learner, recruit, novice

beginning (*n.*) **1.** START, opening, outset, commencement *the beginning of the play* ending **2.** creation, birth, origin, invention, rise, conception, SOURCE *The 1950s marked the beginning of rock 'n' roll.*

behavior (*n.*) CONDUCT, manner, deportment, ATTITUDE, demeanor, carriage

believe (*v.*) TRUST, ACCEPT, ADMIT disbelieve **swallow hook, line, and sinker**

belong (*v.*) FIT, SUIT, befit, pertain

bend (*v.*) TURN, fold, flex, crease, hinge straighten

best (*adj.*) greatest, highest, utmost, supreme, CHIEF, paramount worst

bet (*v.*) RISK, GAMBLE, wager **put money on**

better (*adj.*) **1.** superior, preferable, improved, greater *look for a better job* worse, INFERIOR **2.** healthier, improving, recovering, mending *She's feeling better now that the surgery is over.* worse

big (*adj.*) **1.** LARGE, GREAT, HUGE, bulky, massive *a big dog* SMALL, LITTLE **2.** IMPORTANT, significant, influential, OUTSTANDING, momentous *a big moment in history* UNIMPORTANT, insignificant

bill (*n.*) **1.** beak, nib *the bill of a pelican* **2.** tab, statement, invoice, account *The school paid the bill for the new band uniforms.* **3.** LAW, amendment, measure, proposal *He presented the bill to student government.*

bit (*n.*) PIECE, SCRAP, speck, mite, particle

◆ **Guess the Idiom** ◆

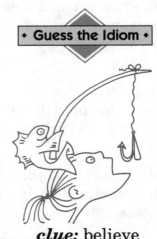

clue: believe

answer: swallow hook, line, and sinker

bite *(v.)* gnaw, nibble, CHEW, grind

bitter *(adj.)* SOUR, SHARP, HARSH, acrid **sweet**

blame *(v.)* ACCUSE, CHARGE, CONDEMN, DISAPPROVE, convict, CRITICIZE, denounce, chide, rebuke, SCOLD
point a finger at

bland *(adj.)* tasteless, STALE, flat, DULL, tedious **tasty,** SPICY

blank *(n.)* SPACE, void, cavity, HOLE

blank *(adj.)* **1.** EMPTY, vacant *fill in the blank space* FULL
2. bewildered, dazed, confused, astonished *a blank stare*

bleak *(adj.)* **1.** DREARY, DISMAL, cheerless, rainy *It was a bleak day yesterday.* BRIGHT, **sunny**
2. BARE, barren *a bleak landscape* **lush**

blend *(v.)* MIX, COMBINE, merge, mingle SEPARATE

block *(v.)* hinder, hamper, STOP, obstruct, thwart, impede, oppose, annul, counteract PASS, ALLOW

blow *(v.)* **1.** fan, ruffle *Blow your hair dry.* **2.** BOTCH, BUNGLE, flub, fumble, goof *blow the exam*

blue *(adj.)* **1.** azure, sapphire, navy, aquamarine, turquoise *She wore a blue dress.* **2.** SAD, GLUM, depressed *feeling blue*
HAPPY
BLEW

blunder *(n.)* MISTAKE, ERROR, slip, oversight

board *(n.)* **1.** plank, WOOD, beam, girder, rafter, timber *Saw the board.* **2.** COMMITTEE, council *The Board of Education oversees the school system.*
BORED

boast *(v.)* BRAG, crow, flaunt, show off
blow one's own horn

body *(n.)* **1.** trunk, torso *The arms extend from the body.*
2. corpse, carcass, cadaver, remains *dissect the body of the frog* **3.** TROOP, COMPANY, BAND, association *She is the president of the student body.*

bold *(adj.)* BRAVE, courageous, unafraid, FEARLESS, VALIANT, intrepid, DARING, CONFIDENT
bashful, SHY

boo *(v.)* hiss, scorn, RIDICULE, DISAPPROVE, deride APPLAUD, PRAISE

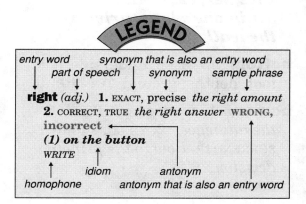

LEGEND

entry word   synonym that is also an entry word
part of speech   synonym   sample phrase

right *(adj.)* **1.** EXACT, precise *the right amount*
2. CORRECT, TRUE *the right answer* WRONG, incorrect
(1) on the button
WRITE

homophone   idiom   antonym   antonym that is also an entry word

boost (v.) **1.** LIFT, RAISE, ELEVATE, hoist *Boost the child up onto the pony.* **2.** expand, INCREASE *boost sales*

border (n.) boundary, EDGE, verge, brink, margin, fringe
BOARDER

bored (adj.) indifferent, disinterested, apathetic **interested, involved, absorbed**
BOARD

boring (adj.) DULL, uninteresting, tiresome, wearisome, humdrum, tedious, monotonous
INTERESTING

boss (n.) director, superintendent, overseer, supervisor, manager

botch (v.) blunder, misjudge, OVERLOOK, SLIP, flub
put one's foot in one's mouth, bark up the wrong tree

bother (n.) TROUBLE, NUISANCE, annoyance, PEST, WORRY
pain in the neck

bother (v.) TEASE, ANNOY, UPSET, IRRITATE, pester, nag, DISTURB, disconcert, harass, torment, provoke, vex, exasperate
get in one's hair, drive up the wall

bottom (n.) BASE, underside, sole, foot, depths, ground TOP, **head**

bow (v.) **1.** BEND, stoop *Bow for the audience.* **2.** YIELD, submit, SURRENDER *Bow to the principal's decision.*
BOUGH

box (n.) CHEST, CASE, carton, bin, trunk, crate, parcel, package, hamper, vault

brace (v.) SUPPORT, prop, bolster, buttress, fortify, stiffen, steady

brag (v.) BOAST, crow, gloat, flaunt
toot one's own horn, pat oneself on the back

brains (n.) INTELLIGENCE, intellect, SENSE, REASON, JUDGMENT

branch (n.) **1.** bough, limb, shoot, offshoot, STICK *the branch of a tree* **2.** department, PART, portion, SECTION *a branch of the government*

◆ **Guess the Idiom** ◆

clue: bother

answer: drive up the wall

brave (adj.) courageous, FEARLESS, DARING, heroic, VALIANT, GALLANT, adventurous, dauntless, intrepid, undaunted COWARDLY

brawl (n.) FIGHT, STRUGGLE, clash, disturbance, tumult

break (v.) **1.** CRACK, snap, FRACTURE, SPLIT, rupture *break your leg* REPAIR **2.** violate, infringe, trespass, transgress *break the law* OBEY **3.** INTERRUPT, STOP, SEPARATE *break the connection* CONNECT, ATTACH *BRAKE*

breathe (v.) inhale, exhale, INSPIRE, expire, gasp, puff, wheeze, sniff, BLOW

brief (adj.) SHORT, concise, condensed, compact LONG, **lengthy**

bright (adj.) **1.** SMART, CLEVER, INTELLIGENT, keen, gifted, ALERT *a bright student* STUPID **2.** BRILLIANT, radiant, sparkling, glittering *a bright light* DIM **3.** vivid *a bright color* DULL

brilliant (adj.) **1.** SMART, INTELLIGENT, BRIGHT, ALERT, gifted, ingenious *a brilliant mind* STUPID, DULL **2.** BRIGHT, sparkling, glittering, SHINY, dazzling *a brilliant star* DIM, DULL

bring (v.) **1.** CARRY, CONVEY, BEAR, DELIVER *Please bring a gift to the party.* **take,** REMOVE **2.** CAUSE, EFFECT, PRODUCE *A rabbit's foot may bring good luck.*

broad (adj.) **1.** WIDE, expansive *Many football players have broad shoulders.* NARROW **2.** comprehensive, extensive, sweeping *Many actors have a broad background in the arts.* limited, **sparse**

bruise (v.) INJURE, HURT, WOUND HEAL

brutal (adj.) CRUEL, MEAN, beastly, savage, fierce, brutish, barbarous KIND, **humane**

budge (v.) stir, shift, MOVE, GO, advance, proceed, progress

build (v.) MAKE, CONSTRUCT, erect, ASSEMBLE, RAISE, fabricate DESTROY

building (n.) structure, edifice, construction

bully (n.) tyrant, ruffian, brute, thug, RASCAL, heavy

bully (v.) FORCE, coerce, intimidate, harass, THREATEN, TEASE

bunch (n.) GROUP, bundle, bale, cluster, COLLECTION, SET, PACK

bungle (v.) BOTCH, fumble, bumble, muddle, muff, blunder, SPOIL

burglar (n.) THIEF, ROBBER, intruder

burn (v.) singe, char, scorch, sear, blister, roast, scald

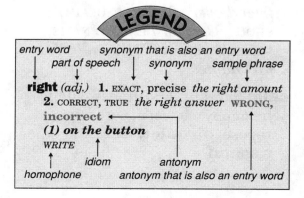

burst (v.) snap, rupture, EXPLODE

bury (v.) inter, PLANT, HIDE, CONCEAL UNCOVER, **reveal**

business (n.) **1.** TRADE, occupation, profession, employment, calling, CAREER, pursuit *She started a new business.* **2.** MATTER, CONCERN, affair, INTEREST *He made it his business to learn all the facts.*

busy (adj.) ACTIVE, LIVELY, hectic, hardworking, industrious, diligent **passive**, IDLE
a finger in every pie

buy (v.) PURCHASE, ACQUIRE, GET, OBTAIN, invest SELL
BY

Cc

• •

cabin (n.) hut, hovel, SHACK, shed, lodge

calculate (v.) compute, COUNT, reckon

call (v.) **1.** summon, INVITE *Call a friend over.* **2.** CRY, EXCLAIM, SHOUT *Call for help.* **3.** NAME, term, christen *Call him by his nickname.*

calm (n.) QUIET, stillness, silence, harmony, concord, serenity, repose **disquiet, unrest, turmoil**

calm (v.) placate, pacify, appease **disrupt,** DISTURB

calm (adj.) **1.** QUIET, STILL, serene, placid, tranquil, restful, PEACEFUL, SMOOTH *a calm day* LOUD, **disruptive 2.** composed, collected, unruffled, restrained, dispassionate *a calm mood* **unrestrained**

cancel (v.) ERASE, delete, nullify, repeal, revoke, annul, obliterate, abolish

capital (n.) **1.** city, metropolis, municipality *the state's capital* **2.** cash, MONEY, funding, WEALTH, resources, assets, means, investment *raise the capital to build a new gym*
CAPITOL

capital (adj.) GOOD, EXCELLENT, first-rate, FINE, CHOICE BAD, **third-rate**

captain (n.) commander, CHIEF, LEADER, skipper

capture (v.) **1.** seize, TAKE, arrest, CATCH, apprehend, TRAP, snare, occupy *The police will capture the thief.* RELEASE, FREE **2.** ATTRACT, captivate, enthrall, charm *Our play will capture the audience's attention.*

car (n.) VEHICLE, motorcar, automobile, carriage

care (n.) safeguard, precaution, forethought, prudence, wariness

care (v.) nurture, foster, CHERISH, nourish

career *(n.)* JOB, profession, occupation, field

careful *(adj.)* CAUTIOUS, attentive, watchful, wary, conscientious, prudent, meticulous, precise, vigilant, discreet, scrupulous CARELESS

walking on eggshells

♦ Guess the Idiom ♦

clue: careful

....

answer: walking on eggshells

careless *(adj.)* negligent, heedless, rash, RECKLESS, inadvertent, accidental, inconsiderate CAREFUL

cargo *(n.)* LOAD, freight

carry *(v.)* BEAR, BRING, TRANSPORT, CONVEY, CONDUCT

cart *(n.)* wagon, vehicle, dray, wheelbarrow

carve *(v.)* CUT, chisel, sculpt, engrave, score, hack, hew, dissect

case *(n.)* **1.** BOX, capsule, covering, sheath *a case for the camera* **2.** occurrence, instance, ACTION,

lawsuit *the case of the missing jewels*

cast *(v.)* **1.** THROW, FLING, sling, lob, hurl, pitch, toss *cast pennies into the fountain* **2.** radiate, spread, emit *use a candle to cast light*

castle *(n.)* **1.** palace, mansion, chateau *The queen lives in a castle.* **2.** fort, fortress, citadel *defend the castle*

catch *(v.)* nab, seize, grasp, snatch, grapple, CAPTURE, arrest, entrap, ensnare, apprehend RELEASE, DROP

category *(n.)* CLASS, SORT, KIND

cause *(n.)* REASON, motive, PURPOSE, incentive, AIM, stimulus EFFECT, RESULT

cause *(v.)* provoke, incite, PRODUCE, CREATE, kindle, originate

caution *(n.)* CARE, heed, wariness, discretion, prudence

caution *(v.)* WARN, ALERT, INFORM, SIGNAL, forewarn, counsel

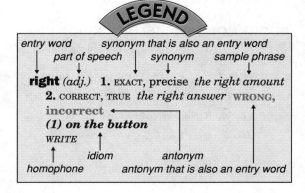

cautious (*adj.*) CAREFUL, prudent, wary, watchful, mindful, circumspect CARELESS, RECKLESS

cave (*n.*) cavern, den, burrow, grotto, HOLE

cease (*v.*) STOP, desist, END, QUIT, refrain, suspend, terminate, FINISH START, BEGIN

celebrate (*v.*) rejoice, HONOR, OBSERVE, PRAISE, extol, revel **disregard, IGNORE**

center (*n.*) MIDDLE, inner, CORE, heart SIDE, BORDER, **outskirts**

ceremony (*n.*) ritual, rite, service, observance, pomp

certain (*adj.*) SURE, SECURE, POSITIVE, assured, convinced, unfailing **uncertain, doubtful** *in the bag*

chain (*v.*) shackle, fetter, manacle, handcuff

challenge (*n.*) **1.** summons, dare *I interpreted his look as a challenge.* **2.** TASK *Studying for the history test was quite a challenge.*

challenge (*v.*) protest, OBJECT, dispute, DEFY, DARE

champion (*n.*) HERO, victor, winner, conqueror, master **loser**

chance (*n.*) **1.** opportunity, occasion, prospect *the chance to succeed* **2.** RISK, HAZARD *take a chance* **certainty**

chance (*adj.*) RANDOM, lucky, accidental, coincidental, fortuitous, serendipitous **contrived, intentional**

change (*v.*) **1.** alter, VARY, revise, ADJUST, amend, modify, update, alternate, ADAPT, edit, reform, convert, transform *change the menu in the cafeteria* **2.** replace, SUBSTITUTE, EXCHANGE *change your clothes before gym class* *(1)* **turn over a new leaf**

character (*n.*) REPUTATION, disposition

characteristic (*n.*) trait, feature, peculiarity, QUALITY

charge (*n.*) **1.** PRICE, COST *What's the charge for the equipment?* **2.** ATTACK, assault *The team captain led the charge.* **3.** accusation *He was jailed on a charge of robbery.*

charge (*v.*) **1.** ATTACK, assault *Charge the fort.* **2.** ACCUSE, BLAME *charge with the crime*

charming (*adj.*) enchanting, bewitching, engaging, fascinating, pleasing, winning

chase (*v.*) HUNT, FOLLOW, track, pursue

cheap (*adj.*) **1.** INEXPENSIVE, low-priced, worthless *a cheap meal* EXPENSIVE **2.** INFERIOR *made of cheap material* **quality, VALUABLE 3.** thrifty, frugal, sparing, STINGY, tightfisted, TIGHT *too cheap to pay* GENEROUS *CHEEP*

cheat *(v.)* swindle, FOOL, DECEIVE, TRICK, mislead, defraud, dupe, hoodwink, delude

check *(v.)* **1.** REVIEW, INSPECT, EXAMINE, monitor, CONFIRM, audit *Check the answers.* **2.** STOP, hinder, curb, obstruct, HALT, restrain *The vaccine will check the spread of the disease.* ALLOW

cheer *(v.)* **1.** APPLAUD, CLAP, salute, root, SUPPORT *Cheer for your favorite team.* BOO **2.** COMFORT, ENCOURAGE, hearten, console *Cheer the team by showing your support.*

cheerful *(adj.)* GLAD, LIVELY, joyful, HAPPY, jolly, MERRY, jubilant, ecstatic SAD

cherish *(v.)* VALUE, treasure, PRIZE, SUPPORT

chest *(n.)* **1.** trunk, torso *The Boy Scout wore a medal on his chest.* **2.** BOX, CASE, trunk, coffer *a treasure chest of coins and jewels*

chew *(v.)* BITE, gnaw, munch, nibble

chief *(n.)* LEADER, chieftain, commander, head, BOSS

chief *(adj.)* MAIN, head, leading, principal, primary

children *(n.)* kids, YOUTH, YOUNG, offspring, juveniles

chill *(v.)* cool, FREEZE, refrigerate

chilly *(adj.)* COLD, COOL, brisk, frigid, frosty HOT, WARM

Go **CRAZY** with **WORDS!**

cheerful

CHEERFUL
HAPPY
JUBILANT
ECSTATIC

chip (*n.*) flake, splinter, sliver

choice (*n.*) selection, pick, option, decision

choice (*adj.*) select, FINE, superior, preferred

choke (*v.*) **1.** suffocate, gasp, stifle, smother, strangle, asphyxiate *choke on a chicken bone* **2.** limit, constrict *The weeds might choke the flowers.*

choose (*v.*) PICK, DECIDE, NAME, select, pluck, appoint, PREFER, nominate, elect, designate *weed out*

chop (*v.*) CUT, mince, dice

chubby (*adj.*) plump, stocky, FAT, fleshy, corpulent SKINNY, THIN

circle (*n.*) RING, halo, hoop, BAND, loop

claim (*n.*) demand, RIGHT, title, assertion

claim (*v.*) DEMAND, REQUIRE, assert, DECLARE

clap (*v.*) APPLAUD, CHEER, PRAISE *give a hand*

class (*n.*) GROUP, CATEGORY, SECTION, department, RANK, ORDER, GRADE, SET, species

clean (*v.*) WASH, WIPE, mop, swab, purify, refine **soil** *straighten up*

clean (*adj.*) spotless, PURE, IMMACULATE, sterile, sanitary, hygienic DIRTY, SOILED, FILTHY *spic-and-span*

clear (*v.*) **1.** REMOVE *Clear the snow from the driveway.* **2.** ERASE, void, vindicate, exonerate, absolve *a chance to clear himself*

clear (*adj.*) **1.** transparent, see-through *clear water* **murky, opaque 2.** OBVIOUS, definite, PLAIN, SURE, apparent, evident *a clear victory* **questionable, unclear 3.** decipherable, graphic, lucid *a clear explanation* **ambiguous,** VAGUE **4.** cloudless, sunny *a clear sky* **5.** BARE, OPEN, denuded *a clear path* **blocked, obstructed**

clever (*adj.*) SMART, QUICK, WISE, WITTY, shrewd, ingenious, deft, skillful, apt SLOW, CLUMSY, **incompetent** *on the ball, sharp as a tack*

• Guess the Idiom •

clue: clever

answer: sharp as a tack

cliff (*n.*) precipice, crag, bank, bluff

climb (*v.*) scale, RISE, mount, clamber, ascend DESCEND

cling (*v.*) **1.** STICK, adhere, HOLD *Lint often clings to fabric.*
2. embrace, clasp *cling to one's doll*

clip (*v.*) CUT, trim, snip, DIVIDE, SEPARATE

close (*v.*) SHUT, slam, LOCK, BAR, FASTEN, secure OPEN

close (*adj.*) **1.** NEAR, nearby, adjacent, adjoining, neighboring, proximate *His house is close to school.* FAR, **distant, removed**
2. immediate, imminent, impending *The date for our vacation is close.* **remote**
3. chummy, FAMILIAR *She's a close friend.* **aloof**
(1) *just a stone's throw away*

cloth (*n.*) MATERIAL, fabric, textile

clothes (*n.*) clothing, garment, attire, habit, outfit, SUIT, costume, frock, garb, uniform, apparel, wardrobe

cloudy (*adj.*) **1.** overcast, shadowy, GLOOMY, DIM *a cloudy day* **sunny, cloudless 2.** blurred, indistinct, VAGUE, unclear, obscure *a cloudy memory* CLEAR
3. murky, opaque *cloudy water* **transparent**

clue (*n.*) HINT, SIGN, EVIDENCE, trace, suggestion, indication

clumsy (*adj.*) AWKWARD, blundering, ungainly, gawky, inept,
cumbersome **dexterous, deft *all thumbs***

clutter (*n.*) MESS, disorder, disarray, jumble **arrangement, array**

coach (*v.*) INSTRUCT, TRAIN, DRILL, prompt

coarse (*adj.*) ROUGH, CRUDE FINE *COURSE*

coast (*n.*) shore, BEACH, seaside, seashore

coax (*v.*) PERSUADE, CONVINCE, INVITE, ATTRACT, wheedle, cajole

coincidence (*n.*) CHANCE, ACCIDENT, fluke

cold (*adj.*) **1.** CHILLY, chilled, COOL, brisk, frosty, icy, wintry, freezing, raw, arctic, frigid *a cold day* HOT **2.** UNFRIENDLY, distant, aloof *a cold attitude* **welcoming,** FRIENDLY

collapse (*v.*) FALL, founder, disintegrate

collect (*v.*) GATHER, ASSEMBLE, harvest, hoard, muster, amass, accumulate SCATTER

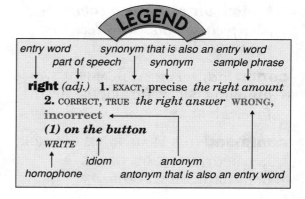

LEGEND

entry word · synonym that is also an entry word
part of speech · synonym · sample phrase

right (*adj.*) **1.** EXACT, precise *the right amount*
2. CORRECT, TRUE *the right answer* WRONG, **incorrect** ←
(1) *on the button*
WRITE
homophone · idiom · antonym · antonym that is also an entry word

collection (n.) **1.** GROUP, cluster, gathering, hoard, store, PILE, accumulation, assortment *He has a great compact disc collection.* **2.** offering, DONATION, CONTRIBUTION, charity *They took up a collection to help the tornado victims.*

college (n.) university, institute, SCHOOL

color (n.) hue, tint, shade, DYE, tone, tinge, pigment, complexion

combat (n.) FIGHT, battle, conflict, skirmish, CONTEST

combat (v.) RESIST, FIGHT, oppose, battle, contend

combine (v.) JOIN, unite, pool, BLEND, MIX, CONNECT SEPARATE

come (v.) ARRIVE, REACH GO, LEAVE

comfort (n.) EASE, RELIEF, PEACE, REST **discomfort**

comfort (v.) CHEER, reassure, console, SOOTHE WORRY, ANNOY, DISTURB

comfortable (adj.) **1.** COZY, comfy, snug *a comfortable chair* **uncomfortable** **2.** EASY, contented, untroubled *a comfortable feeling about the decision* **uneasy, discontented**

comic (adj.) FUNNY, HUMOROUS, amusing, SILLY, HILARIOUS, droll, farcical SERIOUS

command (v.) LEAD, RULE, GOVERN, INSTRUCT, CONTROL, ORDER, dominate OBEY, **comply**

comment (n.) REMARK, statement, utterance, SAYING

comment (v.) EXPRESS, utter, REMARK, react, RESPOND

committee (n.) council, BOARD, commission, GROUP, cabinet

common (adj.) **1.** ORDINARY, commonplace, REGULAR, USUAL, habitual, customary, FREQUENT *Jogging is a common activity.* RARE, **uncommon** **2.** GENERAL, POPULAR, PUBLIC, universal, accepted, prevailing, prevalent *The common opinion is that he's a good president.*
(1) a dime a dozen

communicate (v.) **1.** ANNOUNCE, TELL, disclose, PASS, proclaim, INFORM, impart, reveal *communicate in person* **2.** transmit, CONVEY *communicate over the telephone lines*

community (n.) neighborhood, town, village, district, GROUP, association, society

companion (n.) FRIEND, buddy, mate, comrade, associate

company (n.) **1.** BUSINESS, firm, corporation, partnership, union, alliance *She works at a clothing company.* **2.** guests, visitors *Our company is arriving for dinner at 6:00 P.M.*

compare (v.) liken, match, weigh, relate, equate **contrast**

compete (v.) oppose, rival, contend

competition *(n.)* **1.** CONTEST, rivalry, tournament, MATCH *the tennis competition* **2.** rival, competitor *She's your main competition in the school election.*
(2) *a run for one's money*

complain *(v.)* protest, OBJECT, CHALLENGE, WHINE, moan, groan, mutter, grumble, dispute

complete *(v.)* DO, FINISH, CONCLUDE, accomplish, ACHIEVE, END
wrap up

complete *(adj.)* WHOLE, finished, comprehensive, extensive, BROAD
unfinished, INCOMPLETE

complex *(adj.)* COMPLICATED, tangled, intricate, ELABORATE **CLEAR, PLAIN, SIMPLE**

complicated *(adj.)* DIFFICULT, HARD, COMPLEX, tangled, intricate, convoluted, puzzling, perplexing **SIMPLE, EASY**

compliment *(n.)* PRAISE, HONOR, commendation, endorsement
INSULT
COMPLEMENT

compliment *(v.)* PRAISE, HONOR, commend, FLATTER, congratulate, CELEBRATE **INSULT, OFFEND, dishonor**
sing one's praises
COMPLEMENT

compose *(v.)* **1.** WRITE, CREATE, draft, author, conceive *She composed a short story.* **2.** CALM, CONTROL, COLLECT, QUIET, pacify, quell *He composed himself before speaking to the class.*

comprehend *(v.)* UNDERSTAND, SEE, GET, CONCLUDE, grasp, fathom
get the picture

conceal *(v.)* HIDE, stash, COVER, mask, screen, DISGUISE, BURY, camouflage **uncover, reveal, divulge**

conceited *(adj.)* vain, boastful, smug, arrogant, egotistical, showy, ostentatious, pompous, pretentious, bombastic, grandiose **HUMBLE**
too big for one's britches

• Guess the Idiom •

clue: conceited

answer: too big for one's britches

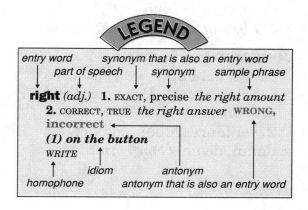

LEGEND

entry word	*synonym that is also an entry word*	
part of speech	*synonym*	*sample phrase*

right *(adj.)* **1.** EXACT, precise *the right amount* **2.** CORRECT, TRUE *the right answer* WRONG, **incorrect** ←
(1) *on the button*
WRITE

homophone · *idiom* · *antonym*
antonym that is also an entry word

concentrate *(v.)* **1.** THINK, ponder, focus *Concentrate on your homework.* **2.** COLLECT, GATHER, consolidate *Concentrate the information in one place.* disperse, DISTRIBUTE **3.** REDUCE, condense, CONTRACT *Concentrate the juice by removing the water.* dilute, THIN

concept *(n.)* IDEA, notion, THOUGHT, theory, impression

concern *(n.)* **1.** MATTER, BUSINESS, PROBLEM, affair, consequence *not your concern* **2.** CARE, WORRY, consideration, regard, THOUGHT, ANXIETY, FEAR *concern for the poor* indifference, apathy

concern *(v.)* **1.** TROUBLE, BOTHER, WORRY, disquiet, preoccupy, DISTURB, perturb *Her behavior concerns her parents.* **2.** AFFECT, INCLUDE, implicate *The situation concerns you.*

conclude *(v.)* **1.** END, FINISH, terminate, CLOSE, complete, CEASE, wrap up *conclude the lesson* BEGIN **2.** determine, deduce, infer, GATHER, REASON, JUDGE, presume, UNDERSTAND *conclude the defendant is innocent* **(1) bring down the curtain**

condemn *(v.)* **1.** BLAME, DISAPPROVE, denounce, CRITICIZE, rebuke, berate *Don't condemn my thinking.* APPLAUD, PRAISE **2.** sentence, JUDGE, convict, damn, doom *Condemn the criminal to life imprisonment.* FORGIVE, PARDON **3.** FORBID, outlaw, proscribe *condemn the actions* SUPPORT, BACK, endorse, ALLOW

condition *(n.)* **1.** STATE, situation *The book is in good condition.* **2.** plight, predicament, illness, SICKNESS *His condition is improving.*

conduct *(n.)* BEHAVIOR, actions, manners, demeanor

conduct *(v.)* **1.** LEAD, DIRECT, GUIDE, MANAGE, GOVERN, OPERATE *Conduct the orchestra.* **2.** GUIDE, LEAD, CONVEY, TRANSPORT, usher *Conduct the child out of the theater.* **3.** ACT, BEHAVE *Conduct yourself in a polite manner.*

confess *(v.)* **1.** TELL, STATE, ADMIT, concede, acknowledge *confess one's guilt* withhold **2.** affirm, avow, profess, DECLARE *He confessed his religious beliefs.*

confidence *(n.)* **1.** self-assurance, assurance, dignity, poise, aplomb *She has confidence in her abilities.* **2.** FAITH, TRUST *place confidence in friendship* DOUBT, apprehension

confident *(adj.)* SURE, assured, CERTAIN, positive, hopeful unsure, doubtful

confidential *(adj.)* SECRET, PRIVATE, restricted, personal, privy

confirm *(v.)* **1.** verify, establish, authenticate, substantiate, validate, ASSURE *confirm a doctor's appointment* **2.** strengthen, fortify, establish, SUPPORT, reinforce, corroborate *confirm an argument* **disprove, refute**

confuse *(v.)* BAFFLE, PUZZLE, bewilder, mystify, confound, mislead, DISTURB **clarify** *throw someone for a loop*

connect *(v.)* JOIN, unite, COMBINE, link, couple SEPARATE, DISCONNECT

conquer *(v.)* BEAT, overcome, subdue, vanquish, quell **succumb, SURRENDER, YIELD**

conscious *(adj.)* **1.** ALIVE, AWAKE, ALERT, AWARE, sensible *She was conscious and breathing after the accident.* **unconscious** **2.** purposeful, intentional *a conscious decision*

conserve *(v.)* PRESERVE, SAVE, KEEP, safeguard, maintain, sustain, support **squander, waste**

consider *(v.)* EXAMINE, STUDY, regard, ponder, muse, REFLECT, speculate, deliberate, JUDGE *turn over in one's mind*

considerate *(adj.)* KIND, WISE, NICE, COURTEOUS, THOUGHTFUL, WARM, discreet, prudent **inconsiderate, THOUGHTLESS, UNKIND**

consistent *(adj.)* CONSTANT, STEADY, REGULAR, unchanging, STABLE, FIRM, uniform **inconsistent, discrepant**

conspicuous *(adj.)* apparent, PLAIN, CLEAR, noticeable, distinct, OBVIOUS, evident, visible, manifest, prominent **inconspicuous** *plain as day, plain as the nose on one's face*

constant *(adj.)* **1.** CONSISTENT, SET, fixed, FIRM, STABLE, REGULAR, unchanging *a constant problem* **intermittent** **2.** FAITHFUL, LOYAL, steadfast, TRUE, DEVOTED *The soldiers remained constant.* **disloyal, traitorous**

construct *(v.)* **1.** BUILD, erect, RAISE, fabricate, MANUFACTURE *construct a model* RAZE **2.** CREATE, forge, FASHION *construct an argument*

consult *(v.)* confer, ADVISE, DISCUSS

contagious *(adj.)* infectious, catching, communicable, transmissible

contain *(v.)* INCLUDE, embody, comprise, HOLD

contaminate *(v.)* POLLUTE, POISON, taint, INFECT, defile, corrupt **purify**

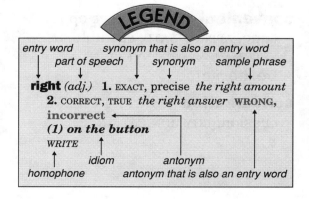

content *(adj.)* satisfied, HAPPY, pleased, appeased **discontented**, UNHAPPY

contest *(n.)* **1.** COMPETITION, GAME, tournament, MATCH *a swimming contest* **2.** STRUGGLE, conflict, rivalry *a contest of wills*

continue *(v.)* persist, endure, MAINTAIN, LAST, persevere **desist**, CEASE
keep the ball rolling

contract *(n.)* agreement, BARGAIN, treaty, DEAL, pact, covenant

contract *(v.)* SHORTEN, LESSEN, DECREASE, diminish, SHRINK, condense EXPAND, **lengthen**

contribute *(v.)* **1.** GIVE, grant, bestow, SUPPLY, DONATE *contribute to charity* **2.** FURNISH, PROVIDE, SUPPLY *contribute your time*

contribution *(n.)* GIFT, DONATION, offering, grant, bestowal

control *(v.)* **1.** DIRECT, MANAGE, dominate, master, COMMAND *The president controls the meeting.* **2.** regulate, curb, CHECK, restrain *control the water flow*

convenient *(adj.)* timely, opportune, APPROPRIATE, suitable, USEFUL, HANDY INCONVENIENT, **bothersome**

conversation *(n.)* TALK, CHAT, discussion, COMMUNICATION

convey *(v.)* **1.** CARRY, BEAR, BRING, TRANSPORT *convey the freight* **2.** COMMUNICATE, divulge, reveal, disclose, transmit *convey the truth*

convince *(v.)* PERSUADE, INFLUENCE, URGE, COAX, goad, spur, induce, entice

cook *(v.)* fry, bake, grill, boil, brew, stew, simmer, broil, sauté, roast, PREPARE

cool *(adj.)* **1.** COLD, CHILLY, brisk *a cool wind* WARM, HOT **2.** UNFRIENDLY, apathetic, unexcited, distant, lukewarm, discourteous, insolent *disappointed by the cool reception* FRIENDLY, **welcoming 3.** GOOD, NEAT, keen *He bought cool sunglasses for the beach.*

cool *(adv.)* CALM, collected, composed NERVOUS, **agitated**

cooperate *(v.)* collaborate, unite **oppose**
put your heads together

copy *(n.)* **1.** DUPLICATE, reproduction, replica *Before turning in his report, he made a copy of it.* **original 2.** imitation, counterfeit, FAKE, phony *They discovered the painting was just a copy of the original.* **original**

copy *(v.)* DUPLICATE, REPRODUCE, mimic, FOLLOW, IMITATE, recreate, transcribe, REPEAT, pirate, ape, impersonate

core *(n.)* **1.** CENTER, MIDDLE *the core of the apple* **2.** essence, heart, gist, substance *the core of the problem*

correct *(v.)* IMPROVE, BETTER, amend, rectify, remedy, revise, reform

correct *(adj.)* **1.** ACCURATE, EXACT, precise *the correct answer* INCORRECT, WRONG **2.** APPROPRIATE, FIT, fitting, JUST, PROPER *correct behavior* IMPROPER *(1) on the nose*

◆ Guess the Idiom ◆

clue: correct

answer: on the nose

corrupt *(adj.)* **1.** dishonest, degenerate, depraved, rotten, villainous, CROOKED, WICKED, EVIL *a corrupt soul* HONEST, MORAL, GOOD **2.** CROOKED, unethical, immoral, shady, double-dealing, unscrupulous, underhanded *a corrupt politician* ethical, scrupulous, upright, dependable, trustworthy

cost *(n.)* PRICE, VALUE, CHARGE, expense, FEE, expenditure

count *(v.)* tally, compute, calculate, ESTIMATE, reckon

country *(n.)* **1.** nation, STATE *Pledge allegiance to your country.* **2.** backwoods, farmland, outback *They lived on a farm in the country.* city

country *(adj.)* RURAL, rustic, pastoral, SIMPLE, PLAIN urban

courage *(n.)* bravery, nerve, daring, valor, pluck, SPIRIT, prowess, fortitude FEAR, COWARDICE, timidity

course *(n.)* **1.** ROUTE, WAY, TRACK, ROAD *a safe course across the mountains* **2.** direction, bearing, itinerary *stay on course* **3.** SUBJECT, program, STUDY, CLASS *She took a biology course.* **4.** process, PLAN, METHOD, procedure *a course of action* COARSE

courteous *(adj.)* POLITE, gracious, obliging, refined, accommodating IMPOLITE, RUDE

cover *(n.)* canopy, roof, SHELTER

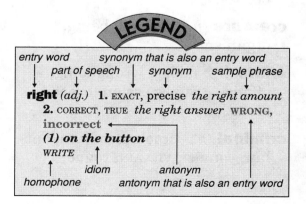

LEGEND

entry word   synonym that is also an entry word
part of speech   synonym   sample phrase

right *(adj.)* **1.** EXACT, precise *the right amount* **2.** CORRECT, TRUE *the right answer* WRONG, incorrect
(1) on the button
WRITE

homophone   idiom   antonym   antonym that is also an entry word

cover (v.) CONCEAL, HIDE, mask, screen, DISGUISE, cloak UNCOVER, EXPOSE, DISPLAY

coward (n.) weakling, chicken, deserter, scaredy-cat HERO

cowardly (adj.) TIMID, shrinking, fearful, AFRAID, BRAVE, heroic, courageous, VALIANT

cozy (adj.) **1.** snug, comfortable, SOFT *a cozy chair* uncomfortable **2.** intimate, FAMILIAR *The room was a cozy setting for a party.* STRANGE, unfamiliar

crack (n.) BREAK, FRACTURE, cleft, fissure, rupture

cram (v.) JAM, SQUEEZE, stuff, gorge, glut, FILL, ram, PRESS, FORCE

crash (n.) collision, impact, ACCIDENT

crash (v.) collide, SMASH, clash

crazy (adj.) MAD, insane, lunatic, demented, deranged SANE
bats in one's belfry

create (v.) MAKE, PRODUCE, FORM, INVENT, render, forge, originate COPY

creature (n.) animal, being, organism

crime (n.) felony, wrongdoing, offense, transgression, breach, violation

criminal (n.) crook, hoodlum, outlaw, convict, VILLAIN, rogue, TRAITOR, renegade, rebel, felon, miscreant, fugitive

critical (adj.) **1.** disapproving, faultfinding, derogatory *a critical speech* uncritical, supportive **2.** DANGEROUS, hazardous, RISKY, precarious, perilous *in critical condition* **3.** CRUCIAL, decisive, IMPORTANT *a critical bit of information* UNIMPORTANT, trivial

criticize (v.) SCOLD, reprimand, chastise, reprove, JUDGE, censor, CONDEMN PRAISE, APPROVE, endorse
tear one to pieces

crooked (adj.) bent, awry, curved, angled, twisted, irregular, asymmetrical, askew STRAIGHT

cross (v.) **1.** span, traverse, REACH, intersect *cross the river* **2.** betray, double-cross *cross the enemy* **3.** CANCEL, STRIKE, MARK *cross it out* **4.** crossbreed, interbreed, hybridize *When you cross an orange with a tangerine, you get a tangelo.*
(2) bite the hand that feeds one

cross (adj.) IRRITABLE, testy, peevish, MOODY, surly, somber, sulky, sullen, morose
a chip on one's shoulder

crouch (v.) squat, stoop, cower, cringe STAND

crowd *(n.)* MOB, multitude, swarm, throng, horde

crucial *(adj.)* SEVERE, trying, decisive, acute, distressing

crude *(adj.)* IMPOLITE, COARSE, RAW, unpolished, RUDE, vulgar POLITE, **well-mannered**

cruel *(adj.)* ruthless, merciless, heartless, BRUTAL, SAVAGE **merciful**

crumble *(v.)* DECAY, decompose, disintegrate, degenerate, deteriorate

crush *(v.)* **1.** SMASH, pound, compress, pulverize *Crush the nut with the nutcracker.* **2.** overpower, CONQUER, subdue, stifle, suppress *crush a rebellion*

cry *(v.)* **1.** WEEP, sob, tear, wail, whimper, WHINE, snivel, blubber, bawl, mourn, grieve, lament *Cry when you are sad.* LAUGH, SMILE **2.** CALL, SHOUT, squeal *Cry for help.*

cuddle *(v.)* HUG, embrace, snuggle, caress, nuzzle

cunning *(adj.)* crafty, skillful, artful, SLY, wily, shrewd, foxy **naive, SIMPLE**

cure *(n.)* remedy, treatment, antidote

cure *(v.)* HEAL, TREAT, remedy, restore, preserve

curious *(adj.)* **1.** inquisitive, investigative, prying, NOSY *She was curious about the customs of other countries.* **detached, uninterested, unresponsive 2.** STRANGE, UNUSUAL, ODD, peculiar, bizarre, UNIQUE *a curious happening in the old house*

curse *(v.)* SWEAR, cuss, blaspheme **bless**

custom *(n.)* tradition, HABIT, ritual, practice, routine, usage, folklore, convention

customer *(n.)* purchaser, buyer, patron, client

cut *(n.)* WOUND, gash, laceration

cut *(v.)* CLIP, snip, slice, dissect, sever, cleave, PART, SPLIT, SEPARATE, DISCONNECT, DETACH, DIVIDE, mince, CARVE, whittle, chisel, engrave, CHOP, hew, crop, hack, lance, prune, trim

cute *(adj.)* adorable, delightful, appealing, DAINTY

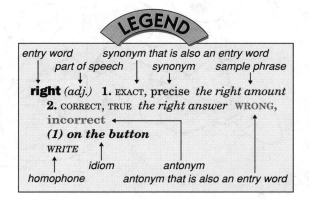

LEGEND

entry word   synonym that is also an entry word
   part of speech   synonym   sample phrase

right *(adj.)* **1.** EXACT, precise *the right amount* **2.** CORRECT, TRUE *the right answer* WRONG, **incorrect**

(1) on the button

WRITE

    idiom   antonym
homophone   antonym that is also an entry word

Dd

dainty *(adj.)* DELICATE, elegant, fragile, petite, frail

damage *(n.)* injury, HARM, MISCHIEF, ruin

damage *(v.)* HARM, INJURE, impair, spoil, RUIN, ABUSE REPAIR, FIX

damp *(adj.)* WET, moist, dank, humid, soaked, drenched DRY

dance *(n.)* prom, BALL, ballet

danger *(n.)* HAZARD, peril, RISK, jeopardy, threat SAFETY, security
thin ice

dangerous *(adj.)* hazardous, risky, unsafe, DIFFICULT, perilous, jeopardous, formidable, precarious SAFE, SECURE, HARMLESS

dare *(v.)* brave, face, CHALLENGE DEFY, risk cower
take the bull by the horns

daring *(adj.)* BRAVE, BOLD, adventurous, FEARLESS, heroic

dark *(adj.)* dim, dusky, shady, shadowy, murky, GLOOMY, overcast, CLOUDY, obscure, opaque LIGHT

Go CRAZY with WORDS!

damp

34

darling *(adj.)* pet, DEAR, beloved, PRECIOUS, cherished, FAVORITE

dash *(v.)* RUSH, HURRY, scurry, scuttle, scamper, SPEED, RACE, bolt, charge **dally, LINGER**

date *(n.)* **1.** engagement, appointment, rendezvous *We went out on a date.* **2.** escort, boyfriend, girlfriend *My date took me to a movie.*

daze *(v.)* dazzle, blind, bewilder, SURPRISE, CONFUSE, stun, AMAZE, stupefy
DAYS

dead *(adj.)* **1.** deceased, lifeless, finished, defunct, EXTINCT *a dead snake* **alive 2.** obsolete, outdated, passé, outmoded *a dead style of clothing*

deadly *(adj.)* **1.** lethal, toxic, poisonous, noxious, malignant, baneful *deadly fumes* **healthful, HEALTHY, wholesome 2.** FATAL, mortal, murderous, lethal *a deadly car accident* **HARMLESS**

deal *(n.)* agreement, treaty, pact, concord, union, trade, negotiation, transaction

deal *(v.)* **1.** TRADE, BARGAIN *deal with another company* **2.** DISTRIBUTE, DIVIDE, allot *Deal the cards.*

dear *(adj.)* **1.** beloved, PRECIOUS, DARLING, cherished, prized *a dear child* **2.** EXPENSIVE, costly, priceless, PRECIOUS, VALUABLE

one of a kind at a dear price
CHEAP, INEXPENSIVE
DEER

debate *(v.)* DISCUSS, argue, dispute, DEMONSTRATE, PROVE, contend, quarrel **agree, concur**

debt *(n.)* due, obligation, liability, deficit

decay *(v.)* ROT, SPOIL, decompose, molder, perish, decline, wither, disintegrate
go to pot

deceive *(v.)* CHEAT, TRICK, FOOL, delude, dupe, hoax, hoodwink, betray, beguile

decide *(v.)* CHOOSE, determine, CONCLUDE, settle **hesitate, vacillate**
make up one's mind

declare *(v.)* SAY, STATE, announce, proclaim, affirm

decorate *(v.)* ADORN, garnish, embellish

decrease *(v.)* LESSEN, diminish, dwindle, wane, REDUCE, curtail
INCREASE

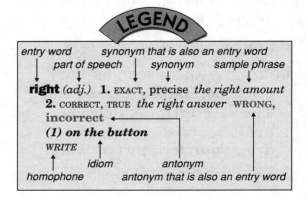

LEGEND

entry word   synonym that is also an entry word
    part of speech   synonym   sample phrase
right *(adj.)* **1.** EXACT, precise *the right amount*
    2. CORRECT, TRUE *the right answer* WRONG,
incorrect
(1) on the button
WRITE
homophone   idiom   antonym
antonym that is also an entry word

deep *(adj.)* **1.** bottomless, abysmal, cavernous *a deep lake* **shallow** **2.** profound, complex *a deep thought* EASY, SIMPLE, CLEAR **3.** SERIOUS, grave, grievous *in deep trouble*

defeat *(v.)* BEAT, OVERTHROW, overcome, CONQUER

defect *(n.)* flaw, blemish, FAULT, weakness, drawback

defect *(v.)* ABANDON, LEAVE, DESERT, forsake, renounce, abscond STAY

defend *(v.)* PROTECT, shield, GUARD, secure ATTACK

defense *(n.)* **1.** protection, GUARD, bulwark *The army provides defense against the enemy.* **offense** **2.** REPLY, ANSWER, retort *She presented her defense in the debate.*

define *(v.)* EXPLAIN, DESCRIBE, clarify, interpret, ascertain

defy *(v.)* RESIST, CHALLENGE, DISOBEY, disregard OBEY

degree *(n.)* **1.** level, GRADE, STEP, STAGE, extent *the degree of danger* **2.** REWARD, GRADE, HONOR *a degree from college*

delay *(n.)* PAUSE, WAIT, interval

delay *(v.)* PAUSE, WAIT, HESITATE, postpone, slacken, detain, stall, dawdle **continue, proceed, prolong, hasten, expedite** *drag your feet, put on hold, put on ice*

delicate *(adj.)* **1.** DAINTY, frail, TENDER *a delicate child* **2.** precarious, CRITICAL *a delicate situation* **3.** subtle, slight *a delicate scent*

delicious *(adj.)* tasty, luscious, juicy, palatable, savory **tasteless, flavorless, BLAND**

delight *(n.)* JOY, happiness, enjoyment, gladness, PLEASURE, ecstasy DISAPPOINTMENT

delight *(v.)* **1.** PLEASE, entice, ATTRACT, captivate *delight the child with stories* **displease, disgust** **2.** SATISFY, enliven *delight the senses*

deliver *(v.)* **1.** SEND, transfer, CONVEY, PASS, DIRECT *deliver a letter* **2.** PRONOUNCE, EXPRESS, ADVANCE, COMMUNICATE *deliver a speech*

demand *(v.)* REQUIRE, ORDER, COMMAND, summon

◆ Guess the Idiom ◆

clue: delay

answer: put on ice

demonstrate *(v.)* **1.** SHOW, ILLUSTRATE, DISPLAY, EXHIBIT *demonstrate the science experiment* CONCEAL, HIDE, DISGUISE, **camouflage 2.** PROVE, TEST, TRY, authenticate, validate *The attorneys will demonstrate that the defendant is innocent.*

dense *(adj.)* **1.** THICK, compact, CLOSE, crowded, lush, impenetrable *a dense forest* **sparse 2.** STUPID, DULL, FOOLISH, IGNORANT, moronic, thick-headed *a dense person* QUICK, INTELLIGENT, BRIGHT

deny *(v.)* **1.** disclaim, renounce, repudiate, refute, DISMISS *Don't deny you're at fault.* **admit, acknowledge 2.** REFUSE, decline *Deny the request.* **grant, permit, allow**

depart *(v.)* **1.** LEAVE, GO, part *Depart on the next plane.* ARRIVE **2.** DIE, PASS, perish, expire *depart from this life*

depend *(v.)* rely, TRUST

depressed *(adj.)* SAD, dejected, GLOOMY, discouraged, disheartened, BLUE, melancholy HAPPY, **joyous**

descend *(v.)* FALL, SINK, DROP, plunge, slip RISE, **ascend**

describe *(v.)* EXPLAIN, clarify, DEFINE, interpret, recount, relate, report, narrate

desert *(v.)* LEAVE, forsake, ABANDON, QUIT, DEFECT, EVACUATE
bail out
DESSERT

deserve *(v.)* EARN, merit, entitle, warrant

desire *(n.)* WISH, NEED, longing, craving

desire *(v.)* WISH, WANT, crave, covet
set your heart on

desperate *(adj.)* hopeless, despondent, despairing, forlorn

despise *(v.)* HATE, detest, scorn, spurn, disdain LIKE, LOVE

destination *(n.)* GOAL, target, END, objective

destroy *(v.)* RUIN, RAZE, demolish, sack, ravage, annihilate, devastate, eradicate, exterminate CREATE

detach *(v.)* SEPARATE, SPLIT, disjoin, DISCONNECT, sever, DIVIDE ATTACH

detail *(n.)* feature, PART, aspect, trait, particular

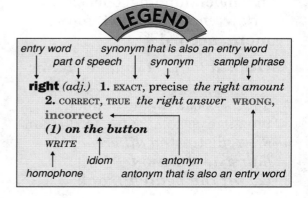

detect (v.) FIND, DISCOVER, SPOT, expose, catch, ascertain

determined (adj.) firm, decided, resolved, resolute, steadfast, relentless

develop (v.) **1.** GROW, CHANGE, mature, evolve *develop into an adult* **2.** EXPAND, INCREASE, promote *develop skills* **3.** CREATE, formulate, synthesize *develop a plan*

device (n.) INSTRUMENT, MACHINE, GADGET, TOOL, apparatus, contraption

devoted (adj.) **1.** FAITHFUL, dutiful, devout, LOYAL, CONSTANT, ardent *a devoted fan* **unfaithful, disloyal 2.** loving, affectionate, attentive *a devoted parent*

die (v.) expire, CEASE, perish, decease LIVE, **survive**
bite the dust, kick the bucket
DYE

difference (n.) **1.** contrast, variation, distinction, diversity *the difference between two colors* **similarity 2.** disagreement, misunderstanding, opposition *a difference of opinion* **agreement, accord**

different (adj.) **1.** unlike, dissimilar, varying, diverse *different habits* SAME **2.** uncommon, UNUSUAL, SPECIAL, ODD, EXTRAORDINARY, distinct *a different hairstyle* COMMON
(2) *off the beaten track*

difficult (adj.) HARD, trying, COMPLICATED, COMPLEX, tangled, intricate, arduous, laborious, formidable, irksome EASY, SIMPLE
easier said than done, no picnic, an uphill climb

• Guess the Idiom •

clue: difficult

answer: an uphill climb

dig (v.) burrow, hollow, scoop, mine, quarry, excavate, delve

dilapidated (adj.) decayed, ruined, SHABBY, run-down, deteriorated, neglected, unkempt

dim (adj.) DARK, DULL, shadowy, FAINT, unclear, WEAK, obscure, VAGUE, indistinct, faded BRIGHT

dine (v.) EAT, consume, feast, gorge

dingy (n.) DIRTY, soiled, sullied, dull, dusky CLEAN

direct (v.) ORDER, COMMAND, INSTRUCT, AIM, POINT, SHOW
call the shots

directions (n.) instructions, formula, prescription, GUIDE, COURSE

dirt *(n.)* soil, earth, land, GROUND, mud, muck, dust, sediment, grime, soot

dirty *(adj.)* **1.** unclean, FILTHY, soiled, grimy, impure, FOUL, vile, GROSS, contaminated, polluted, squalid *dirty water* PURE, CLEAN **2.** obscene, indecent, smutty, offensive *dirty language*
(2) off-color

disadvantage *(n.)* handicap, drawback, obstacle, hindrance, inconvenience ADVANTAGE

disagree *(v.)* REJECT, oppose, CHALLENGE, DENY, dispute AGREE, **concur**

disappear *(v.)* VANISH, FADE, evaporate, DISSOLVE, vaporize APPEAR

disappoint *(v.)* dissatisfy, FRUSTRATE, foil, FAIL PLEASE

disappointment *(n.)* frustration, setback, FAILURE, DEFEAT, unfulfillment, dissatisfaction

disapprove *(v.)* REJECT, CONDEMN, censure, OBJECT, oppose, protest, dispute APPROVE, ACCEPT
take a dim view of, take exception to

disaster *(n.)* mishap, misfortune, mischance, tragedy, catastrophe, calamity

discard *(v.)* REJECT, scrap, eliminate, exclude, jettison KEEP, **retain**

disconnect *(v.)* SEPARATE, disjoin, sever, DETACH, disengage CONNECT

discourage *(v.)* **1.** dishearten, depress, deject, unnerve *The high cost of supplies will discourage us.* encourage **2.** dissuade, deter, obstruct, inhibit, BLOCK, prevent *Placing land mines will discourage the advance of the enemy.*
(2) throw cold water on

discover *(v.)* FIND, reveal, UNCOVER, LEARN

discuss *(v.)* TALK, negotiate, deliberate

disease *(n.)* SICKNESS, ailment, malady

disgrace *(n.)* disfavor, SHAME, dishonor, infamy, scandal, contempt, humiliation HONOR

disgrace *(v.)* defile, SHAME, smirch HONOR
drag through the mud

disguise *(n.)* costume, mask, guise, camouflage

disguise *(v.)* masquerade, CONCEAL, mask, HIDE, camouflage

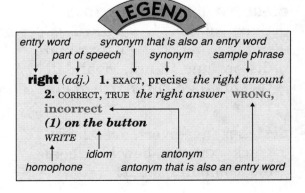

LEGEND

entry word   *synonym that is also an entry word*
    part of speech   *synonym*   *sample phrase*

right *(adj.)* **1.** EXACT, precise *the right amount* **2.** CORRECT, TRUE *the right answer* WRONG, incorrect
(1) on the button
WRITE   *idiom*   *antonym*
homophone   *antonym that is also an entry word*

disgusting *(adj.)* repulsive, distasteful, offensive, CRUDE, revolting, repellent, loathsome, vulgar

dishonest *(adj.)* lying, untruthful, deceitful, mendacious, CROOKED, CORRUPT, fraudulent, unprincipled HONEST, **truthful two-faced**

dislike *(v.)* disfavor, DISAPPROVE, HATE, loathe, detest LIKE

dismal *(adj.)* cheerless, GLOOMY, DARK, DULL, dreary, depressing

dismiss *(v.)* **1.** fire, DISCHARGE, unseat, RELEASE *dismiss an employee* HIRE, EMPLOY **2.** DISCARD, REJECT, expel, decline *dismiss an idea* ACCEPT, HOLD, **retain, embrace**

disobey *(v.)* DEFY, disregard, IGNORE, neglect, REJECT, rebel, revolt, OFFEND, transgress, infringe OBEY

display *(n.)* **1.** exhibition, exposition, pageant, fanfare *a display of jewelry* **2.** exhibition, SHOW *a display of affection*

display *(v.)* EXHIBIT, SHOW, publicize COVER, HIDE, CONCEAL

dissolve *(v.)* **1.** liquefy, MELT, thaw, soften *The sugar dissolves in hot water.* **2.** END, terminate, discontinue, annul, invalidate, repeal *dissolve a partnership* FORM

distract *(v.)* divert, avert, sidetrack, CONFUSE, bewilder, befuddle, confound, PUZZLE

distress *(n.)* **1.** PAIN, AGONY, anguish, GRIEF, woe, torment *He felt distress over the loss of his job.* **2.** TROUBLE, WORRY, adversity *financial distress* **(1) a heavy heart**

distribute *(v.)* **1.** dispense, allot, issue, disperse, allocate, DIVIDE, apportion *Distribute the funds.* **2.** SCATTER, SPREAD, disperse, sprinkle *Distribute the seeds.* GATHER, COLLECT

disturb *(v.)* INTERRUPT, TROUBLE, disquiet, ALARM, disrupt, unsettle, perturb, disconcert CALM **kick up a storm, rock the boat**

ditch *(n.)* trench, trough, channel, moat, gully

dive *(v.)* plunge, submerge, immerse

divide *(v.)* **1.** SPLIT, CUT, sever, slice, cleave, PART, SEPARATE, rend *The river divides the land.* **unite 2.** SHARE, DISTRIBUTE, apportion *Divide the pizza among the guests.*

divine *(adj.)* **1.** HOLY, RELIGIOUS, blessed, godlike, heavenly, spiritual *a divine experience* **2.** EXCELLENT, delightful, SUPER, admirable *a divine dinner*

dizzy *(adj.)* unsteady, staggering, unstable, hazy, giddy

do (*v.*) PERFORM, FINISH, COMPLETE, enact, ACT, ACHIEVE, commit, execute, EFFECT, perpetrate **undo** *carry out*
DEW, DUE

dodge (*v.*) AVOID, MISS, ESCAPE, evade, elude, hedge

dog (*n.*) hound, canine, pooch, mongrel, mutt, puppy

donation (*n.*) contribution, offering, alms, dole, GIFT, PRESENT, gratuity

door (*n.*) entrance, entry, EXIT, gate, threshold, portal

doubt (*n.*) CONCERN, anxiety, uncertainty, skepticism, distrust **certainty**

doubt (*v.*) QUESTION, distrust, mistrust, SUSPECT, dispute *think something sounds fishy, take with a grain of salt, call into question*

doze (*v.*) SLEEP, slumber, NAP, drowse

drab (*adj.*) DREARY, DULL, DINGY, flat BRIGHT, **vivid**

drag (*v.*) **1.** PULL, haul, DRAW, tug, tow *Drag the cart up the hill.* **2.** LINGER, dawdle, loiter, poke *The day dragged when he had little to do.* **3.** lengthen, EXTEND, prolong *Drag out the argument.* **(2)** *go at a snail's pace*

draw (*v.*) **1.** SKETCH, illustrate, PICTURE, portray, REPRESENT, draft, depict *Draw a picture.* **2.** REMOVE, TAKE *Draw water from the well.* **3.** PULL, drag *Draw the curtains.* **4.** ATTRACT, LEAD, induce, elicit, provoke *draw attention to oneself*

dread (*n.*) FEAR, ALARM, awe, TERROR, apprehension

dream (*n.*) **1.** vision, fantasy, ILLUSION, nightmare *a frightening dream in the middle of the night* **2.** GOAL *Her dream is to be a doctor.*

dreary (*adj.*) **1.** GLOOMY, DARK, DISMAL, cheerless, depressing, forlorn *a dreary day* **sunny,** BRIGHT **2.** BORING, DULL, tedious, tiresome *a dreary time doing yard work*

dress (*n.*) CLOTHES, attire, apparel

drill (*v.*) bore, PIERCE, poke, puncture, perforate, penetrate

drink (*v.*) sip, swallow, gulp *wet your whistle*

drive (*v.*) **1.** GUIDE, OPERATE, DIRECT, CONTROL *drive a car* **2.** FORCE, INFLUENCE, pressure, PRESS, compel *We must drive the committee to make a decision.*

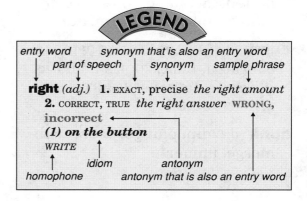

LEGEND

entry word   synonym that is also an entry word
   part of speech | synonym   sample phrase
right (*adj.*) **1.** EXACT, precise *the right amount* **2.** CORRECT, TRUE *the right answer* WRONG, **incorrect**
(1) on the button
WRITE
   idiom   antonym
homophone   antonym that is also an entry word

droop (v.) wither, wilt, FADE, sag, slouch, slump

drop (v.) **1.** FALL, TUMBLE, COLLAPSE *drop to the floor* **2.** lower, REDUCE, decline, dwindle, SINK *Car sales may drop.* INCREASE **3.** OMIT, ELIMINATE, discontinue, ABANDON, forsake, DESERT, REJECT *Drop the project from the schedule.* **adopt, ACCEPT**

drunk (adj.) tipsy, inebriated, intoxicated SOBER

dry (v.) wither, parch, shrivel WET

dry (adj.) parched, barren, waterless, arid, thirsty WET

due (adj.) **1.** owed, unpaid, payable, OUTSTANDING, unsatisfied *Pay the amount due.* **2.** PROPER, FIT, suitable, deserved, warranted *He received due punishment for the crime.* **3.** expected, awaited, anticipated, scheduled *The report is due on Friday.*

dull (adj.) **1.** blunt, WEAK *a dull knife* **2.** BORING, uninteresting, STALE, trite, COMMON, tedious *a dull movie* **INTERESTING, exciting 3.** DIM, flat, DRAB, muted, lackluster *a dull color* **BRIGHT, BRILLIANT, luminous**

dumb (adj.) IGNORANT, STUPID, uneducated, DULL, FOOLISH, idiotic, illiterate, fatuous **SMART, BRIGHT, QUICK**

dunk (v.) dip, plunge, douse, submerge, immerse

duplicate (n.) COPY, reproduction, replica, likeness, twin ORIGINAL

duplicate (v.) COPY, reproduce, imitate, double, REPEAT

duty (n.) **1.** TASK, obligation, responsibility *He felt it was his duty to help the needy.* **2.** tax, toll, CUSTOM *Pay the duty on imported goods.*

dwell (v.) LIVE, INHABIT, occupy, STAY, reside, abide

dye (n.) pigment, tint, COLOR, STAIN, tinge *DIE*

dye (v.) COLOR, tint, STAIN *DIE*

Ee

eager (adj.) ENTHUSIASTIC, zealous, avid, keen, fervent, ardent **reluctant, hesitant**

early (adj.) **1.** timely, premature *an early arrival* LATE **2.** former, previous, preceding, prior *the early years* **latter**

earn (v.) GAIN, GET, ACQUIRE, merit, WIN, DESERVE

earnest (adj.) DETERMINED, ardent, EAGER, fervent, passionate, SINCERE, SERIOUS

ease (*n.*) **1.** REST, repose, QUIET, COMFORT, contentment, HAPPINESS, relaxation, security, well-being *She felt at ease when on vacation.* **discomfort, disquiet, WORRY, vexation, tension** **2.** knack, facility, readiness, effortlessness *She completed the test with ease.* **difficulty**

ease (*v.*) COMFORT, SOOTHE, QUIET, console, relieve, alleviate **worsen, exacerbate**

easy (*adj.*) SIMPLE, effortless, elementary **DIFFICULT**
a piece of cake

◆ Guess the Idiom ◆

clue: easy

....

answer: a piece of cake

eat (*v.*) DINE, consume, devour, munch, CHEW, nibble, swallow, gobble, gorge **abstain, fast**

echo (*v.*) REPEAT, REFLECT, resound, IMITATE, mimic, reverberate

edge (*n.*) BORDER, boundary, LIMIT, brink, brim, RIM, lip, SIDE, verge, margin **CENTER, MIDDLE**

educate (*v.*) TEACH, INSTRUCT, TRAIN, discipline, EXPLAIN, inform, cultivate

effect (*n.*) RESULT, consequence, issue, outcome **CAUSE**

effect (*v.*) PRODUCE, realize, accomplish, induce **CAUSE**

effort (*n.*) **1.** TASK, chore, STRUGGLE, STRAIN *a physical effort* **2.** ATTEMPT, trial, endeavor, undertaking, venture *the athlete's best effort*

elaborate (*adj.*) **1.** decorated, ornate, detailed, intricate *an elaborate design* **PLAIN** **2.** COMPLICATED, involved, DIFFICULT *He tackled the elaborate problem.* **SIMPLE**

elegant (*adj.*) refined, GRACEFUL, polished, FINE, genteel **CLUMSY, unpolished**

elevate (*v.*) **1.** RAISE, LIFT, hoist *Elevate the crane.* **lower, deflate, depress** **2.** promote, upgrade, advance, BOOST, heighten *elevate to a higher-paying job* **demote, downgrade, lower**

eliminate (*v.*) OMIT, REMOVE, expel, exclude, abolish, cancel **INCLUDE**

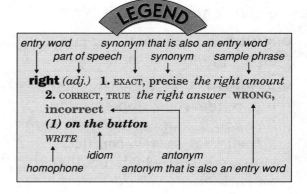

LEGEND

| entry word | synonym that is also an entry word |
| part of speech | synonym | sample phrase |

right (*adj.*) **1.** EXACT, precise *the right amount* **2.** CORRECT, TRUE *the right answer* WRONG, **incorrect** ◄
(1) on the button
WRITE

homophone | idiom | antonym | antonym that is also an entry word

embarrass (*v.*) SHAME, HUMILIATE, degrade, mortify, abash
put down, cause to lose face

• Guess the Idiom •

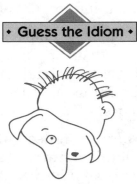

clue: embarrass

answer: cause to lose face

emergency (*n.*) crisis, dilemma, PROBLEM, predicament, difficulty

emotion (*n.*) FEELING, passion, sentiment, impression

employ (*v.*) **1.** HIRE, engage, CONTRACT, enlist, sign up *employ students for the summer* **2.** USE, utilize, wield, apply *employ a new tool for road building*

empty (*adj.*) **1.** unfilled *an empty glass* FULL **2.** vacant, uninhabited, deserted, void *an empty house* occupied **3.** BARE, BLANK, desolate, devoid, barren *an empty landscape* lush

enclose (*v.*) SURROUND, encircle, envelop, WRAP, encompass

encounter (*n.*) **1.** meeting, joining, rendezvous, appointment *She had a chance encounter with a friend.* **2.** BATTLE, conflict, FIGHT, CONTEST, clash, bout, FEUD *an encounter with the enemy*

encounter (*v.*) MEET, confront, FACE AVOID, MISS
run across, stumble upon

encourage (*v.*) **1.** hearten, COMFORT, ASSURE, reassure, revitalize, INSPIRE, embolden *They encouraged the runner to finish the race.* DISCOURAGE, **dishearten** **2.** SUPPORT, foster, advocate, advance *encourage recycling* **oppose, hinder**
(1) give one a shot in the arm

end (*n.*) **1.** LIMIT, boundary *the end of the road* **2.** conclusion, finale, outcome, RESULT *the end of the book* **beginning** **3.** GOAL, PURPOSE *the means to an end*

end (*v.*) STOP, FINISH, lapse, discontinue, COMPLETE, CONCLUDE, CLOSE, CHECK, suspend, arrest, abort, terminate, culminate, annul BEGIN, START, **open**
pull the plug

• Guess the Idiom •

clue: end

answer: pull the plug

44

endanger *(v.)* RISK, DARE, imperil, jeopardize PROTECT

endless *(adj.)* boundless, limitless, infinite, continuous **limited, finite**

enemy *(n.)* FOE, RIVAL, OPPONENT, competitor, antagonist, opposition, adversary FRIEND

energetic *(adj.)* vigorous, ACTIVE, vital, spirited, LIVELY **inactive, LAZY**

energy *(n.)* SPIRIT, vitality, force, STRENGTH, POWER, MIGHT, efficiency, vigor, vim

enhance *(v.)* IMPROVE, INCREASE, enrich, APPRECIATE **detract**

enjoy *(v.)* LIKE, APPRECIATE
have a ball

enlarge *(v.)* GROW, bulge, SWELL, INCREASE, EXPAND, EXTEND, amplify, magnify REDUCE

enormous *(adj.)* HUGE, monstrous, IMMENSE, GIGANTIC, VAST **TINY, minute**

enough *(adj.)* plenty, ADEQUATE, sufficient, ample, FULL, SATISFACTORY, abundant, PLENTIFUL **wanting, lacking, unsatisfactory**

enrage *(v.)* ANGER, madden, infuriate, inflame, vex, AGGRAVATE, provoke
make one's blood boil

enter *(v.)* **1.** penetrate, INVADE, INTRUDE *Enter the abandoned house.* EXIT, LEAVE **2.** inscribe, register, RECORD, INTRODUCE *Enter the information into the computer.* ERASE, **delete**
(1) set foot in

entertain *(v.)* AMUSE, PLEASE, CHEER, divert **bore**

enthusiasm *(n.)* eagerness, INTEREST, fervor, passion, ZEAL **apathy**

enthusiastic *(adj.)* EAGER, avid, passionate, fervent, zealous, ardent, keen, vehement **reluctant**
all fired up

entire *(adj.)* WHOLE, COMPLETE, FULL, intact **partial, INCOMPLETE**

environment *(n.)* surrounding, atmosphere, neighborhood, scene, circumstances

envy *(n.)* jealousy, resentment, covetousness, malice, SPITE

envy *(v.)* covet, begrudge

episode *(n.)* occurrence, incident, circumstance, happening, EVENT, occasion

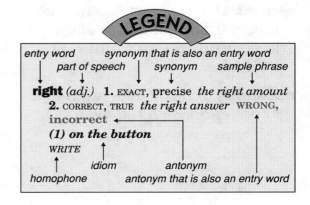

entry word   synonym that is also an entry word
part of speech   synonym   sample phrase

right *(adj.)* **1.** EXACT, precise *the right amount*
2. CORRECT, TRUE *the right answer* WRONG, **incorrect**
(1) on the button
WRITE

homophone   idiom   antonym   antonym that is also an entry word

45

equal *(adj.)* **1.** LIKE, ALIKE, SAME, IDENTICAL, EQUIVALENT, duplicate *They have equal athletic ability.* **unequal, dissimilar 2.** FAIR, impartial, JUST, nondiscriminatory, unbiased *The judge gave equal consideration to both people.* **inequitable, unfair**

equip *(v.)* FURNISH, PROVIDE, arm, rig, SUPPLY, prepare

equipment *(n.)* gear, apparatus, implement, paraphernalia

equivalent *(adj.)* EQUAL, SAME, matching, ALIKE, identical, interchangeable, synonymous **unequivalent, unequal, dissimilar, DIFFERENT**

erase *(v.)* delete, REMOVE, CANCEL, obliterate, nullify, annul ADD

erode *(v.)* corrode, WEAR, abrade

errand *(n.)* mission, TASK, CHORE, JOB, duty, assignment

error *(n.)* MISTAKE, FAULT, shortcoming, failing, fallacy

escape *(v.)* flee, AVOID, evade, elude, abscond
fly the coop

essential *(adj.)* NECESSARY, vital, IMPORTANT, fundamental, key, BASIC **unnecessary, unrequired**

establish *(v.)* **1.** found, originate, START *establish a colony in the New World* **2.** PROVE, SUPPORT, substantiate, verify *He will establish his argument before we ask questions.*
(2) lay the foundation

estimate *(n.)* **1.** approximation, GUESS *His estimate is that the bike is worth about $200.* **2.** appraisal, valuation, PRICE *The mechanic will give us an estimate to repair the damage.*
(1) a ballpark figure

estimate *(v.)* value, appraise, assess, COUNT, APPROXIMATE, round, round off, reckon, calculate

evacuate *(v.)* LEAVE, ABANDON, DESERT, relinquish FILL, **occupy**

◆ **Guess the Idiom** ◆

clue: escape

answer: fly the coop

even *(adj.)* **1.** SMOOTH, LEVEL, FLAT, HORIZONTAL *an even surface* **2.** CALM, placid, unruffled *an even temper* **3.** STEADY, REGULAR, CONSISTENT, unchanging, CONSTANT, unvarying, uniform, monotonous *an even flow of water* **irregular 4.** EQUAL, EQUIVALENT, LIKE *an even score* **uneven, unequal, disparate**

event *(n.)* happening, occasion, occurrence, performance, EPISODE, opportunity, EXPERIENCE, affair, INCIDENT

evidence *(n.)* PROOF, testimony, facts

evil *(adj.)* BAD, WICKED, sinful, sinister, DISHONEST, CROOKED, shady, CORRUPT, IMMORAL, villainous, depraved, unprincipled, unscrupulous **GOOD, MORAL**

exact *(adj.)* CORRECT, precise, ACCURATE, absolute **inexact, APPROXIMATE**
to the letter

exaggerate *(v.)* overstate, MAGNIFY, ENLARGE, amplify **understate**
make a mountain out of a molehill, blow out of proportion

examine *(v.)* INSPECT, analyze, scan, INVESTIGATE, EXPLORE, SEARCH, probe, scrutinize
go over with a fine-tooth comb

• Guess the Idiom •

clue: examine

answer: go over with a fine-tooth comb

example *(n.)* SAMPLE, model, PATTERN, specimen, standard, norm, paradigm

exceed *(v.)* **1.** BEAT, surpass, excel, outpace, top *The cyclist exceeds her opponent by half a mile.* **2.** dominate, outdo *This trial run exceeds my ability.*
(1) leave in the dust

excellent *(adj.)* GREAT, FINE, superior, SUPERB, SPLENDID, MARVELOUS, CHOICE, admirable, EXTRAORDINARY **mediocre, INFERIOR, ORDINARY**

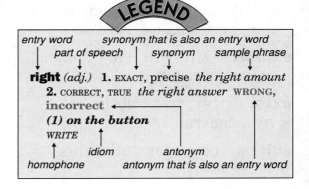

LEGEND

entry word   synonym that is also an entry word
   part of speech   synonym   sample phrase

right *(adj.)* **1.** EXACT, precise *the right amount* **2.** CORRECT, TRUE *the right answer* **WRONG, incorrect**
(1) on the button
WRITE

homophone   idiom   antonym   antonym that is also an entry word

exchange (*v.*) TRADE, swap, barter, SUBSTITUTE, interchange

excite (*v.*) stimulate, provoke, ENCOURAGE, URGE, incite, animate bore

exclaim (*v.*) YELL, SHOUT, CALL, DECLARE, blurt out

exclude (*v.*) BAR, prohibit, OMIT, disallow, FORBID, banish, REJECT, spurn, blackball, DROP INCLUDE

excuse (*n.*) REASON, plea, apology, DEFENSE, justification

excuse (*v.*) **1.** FORGIVE, PARDON, exempt, condone *Please excuse the mistake.* REWARD, PRAISE, PUNISH **2.** FREE, RELEASE *The teacher will excuse us from class.* detain
(1) look the other way

exhaust (*v.*) **1.** expend, USE, DRAIN, consume, SPEND, FINISH *exhaust the food supply* replenish **2.** weaken, FATIGUE, wind, tire, WEAR, tax, sap, strain *The runner exhausted himself.* invigorate, revive
(1) scrape the bottom of the barrel

exhibit (*n.*) exhibition, fair, DISPLAY, SHOW, presentation, exposition, performance, spectacle

exhibit (*v.*) DISPLAY, SHOW, DEMONSTRATE, PRESENT, disclose

exist (*v.*) BE, LIVE, subsist, SURVIVE, BREATHE, abide

exit (*n.*) DOOR, gate entrance

exit (*v.*) LEAVE, GO, DEPART, MOVE, migrate, emigrate ENTER

expand (*v.*) **1.** STRETCH, ENLARGE, INCREASE, SWELL, dilate, distend *Expand the size of the vegetable garden.* CONTRACT **2.** DEVELOP, INCREASE, elaborate, STRENGTHEN, SPREAD, accelerate *expand the business* REDUCE, DECREASE

expect (*v.*) anticipate, await, HOPE

expensive (*adj.*) costly, DEAR, pricey CHEAP, INEXPENSIVE

experience (*n.*) **1.** happening, EVENT *a horrible experience* **2.** PRACTICE, KNOWLEDGE, SKILL, background *He has experience teaching.*

expert (*n.*) authority, master, veteran, specialist BEGINNER, novice

expert (*adj.*) ABLE, experienced, masterful, skillful, competent, deft, proficient amateurish, inept

explain (*v.*) **1.** DESCRIBE, DEFINE, clarify, interpret, TRANSLATE *He explained the assignment to his students.* **2.** SOLVE, decipher, decode, resolve *Try to explain the puzzle.*
(1) spell out

explode (*v.*) BURST, detonate, rupture, erupt

explore (*v.*) SEARCH, INVESTIGATE, probe, INSPECT, EXAMINE

expose (*v.*) **1.** UNCOVER, BARE *expose the wound to the air* COVER, HIDE **2.** DISCOVER, disclose, reveal *expose the truth*

express (*v.*) SPEAK, utter, STATE, TELL, DECLARE

extend (*v.*) **1.** STRETCH, REACH, EXPAND, elongate *extend a cord* **contract, condense 2.** lengthen, prolong *extend a rehearsal* **shorten**

extinct (*adj.*) DEAD, defunct, finished, gone, ended, vanished **living**

extra (*adj.*) additional, surplus, SPARE, reserve, remnant, UNNECESSARY, redundant, excessive, needless, superfluous

extraordinary (*adj.*) **1.** UNUSUAL, uncommon, RARE, ODD, peculiar, bizarre *an extraordinary event* **commonplace, ORDINARY 2.** striking, remarkable, amazing, astonishing, glorious, miraculous, wondrous *the extraordinary beauty of nature* **3.** noteworthy, eminent, IMPORTANT, impressive, exceptional *recognized for one's extraordinary talent*

Ff

● ● ● ● ● ● ● ● ● ● ● ● ● ● ● ●

fabulous (*adj.*) MARVELOUS, SUPERB, GREAT, WONDERFUL, amazing, astounding, remarkable, exceptional, legendary

fact (*n.*) TRUTH, reality, certainty **fiction**

fade (*v.*) **1.** discolor, pale, bleach *The book's paper faded over time.* **2.** weaken, wither, DIE *The flowers faded in the sun.*

fail (*v.*) **1.** flunk, bomb *The student failed the class.* SUCCEED, **triumph 2.** DISAPPOINT, neglect *fail his friends* **3.** weaken, decline, deteriorate *Her health failed.*

failure (*n.*) **1.** DEFEAT, frustration, BLUNDER, ERROR, SLIP *the failure of a business* SUCCESS **2.** loser, lemon, dud *a failure in life* **3.** delinquency, negligence, default, oversight, dereliction *failure to respond to the summons*

faint (*v.*) swoon, COLLAPSE, crumple, DROP

faint (*adj.*) **1.** DIM, PALE, faded, muted, blurred, fuzzy, muffled, mild *a faint signal* **bright 2.** dizzy, woozy, FEEBLE *a faint feeling*

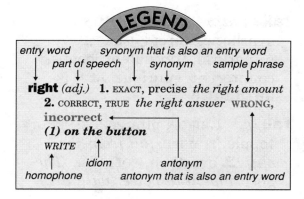

LEGEND

entry word   synonym that is also an entry word
    part of speech   synonym   sample phrase

right (*adj.*) **1.** EXACT, precise *the right amount* **2.** CORRECT, TRUE *the right answer* WRONG, **incorrect** ←
(1) on the button
WRITE

homophone   idiom   antonym
          antonym that is also an entry word

fair *(n.)* exhibition, gathering, exposition, bazaar, FESTIVAL, carnival
FARE

fair *(adj.)* **1.** JUST, unbiased, RIGHT, HONEST, truthful, STRAIGHT, upright, SOUND, lawful, reasonable, impartial, equitable, neutral, rational, virtuous, diligent, conscientious, scrupulous *a fair verdict* **unfair 2.** sunny *fair weather* RAINY **3.** BEAUTIFUL *a fair maiden* UGLY **4.** LIGHT *a fair complexion* DARK
FARE

fairy *(n.)* elf, pixie, sprite, naiad, nymph

faith *(n.)* **1.** belief, TRUST, CONFIDENCE *The jurors showed faith in the judge.* DOUBT **2.** creed, religion, belief, doctrine, persuasion, denomination *free to worship in one's faith*

faithful *(adj.)* trustworthy, LOYAL, TRUE, DEVOTED **unfaithful, traitorous**

fake *(n.)* fraud, forgery, imitation, sham, IMPOSTOR, charlatan **original**

fake *(adj.)* ARTIFICIAL, FALSE, synthetic, unreal, IMAGINARY, unnatural, fraudulent, bogus, counterfeit, spurious REAL, **authentic**

fall *(v.)* **1.** DROP, plunge, DESCEND, topple, TUMBLE *fall from the cliff* **2.** overturn, COLLAPSE *The government in power will fall.*

3. DECREASE, SINK, diminish, REDUCE, subside *The temperature will fall.* INCREASE

false *(adj.)* **1.** UNTRUE, incorrect, WRONG, erroneous, inaccurate *The rumor I heard was false.* TRUE, **factual 2.** counterfeit, FAKE, bogus, spurious *a false gem* GENUINE, **authentic**

fame *(n.)* renown, HONOR, GLORY, repute, distinction, eminence **obscurity**

familiar *(adj.)* CLOSE, FRIENDLY, intimate, COMMON, well-known **unfamiliar**

family *(n.)* relatives, kin, ancestors, clan, tribe

famous *(adj.)* celebrated, well-known, popular, noted, notable, renowned, distinguished, eminent, illustrious, prominent **unknown**

fan *(n.)* admirer, follower, supporter, enthusiast, devotee

fancy *(adj.)* **1.** decorated, ELABORATE, ornate, embellished *a fancy sweater* PLAIN **2.** ELEGANT, FINE, lavish, refined *a fancy restaurant*

fantastic *(adj.)* **1.** INCREDIBLE, WONDERFUL, MARVELOUS *That was a fantastic concert.* **2.** fictitious, fictional, fanciful, IMAGINARY, unreal, unbelievable, incredible, farfetched *a fantastic tale* **realistic**, ORDINARY

far *(adj.)* remote, distant, removed NEAR, CLOSE

fascinate *(v.)* CHARM, enchant, DELIGHT, intrigue, transfix

fashion *(n.)* STYLE, trend, mode, CUSTOM

fashion *(v.)* MAKE, BUILD, CONSTRUCT, PRODUCE, CREATE, FORM, SHAPE

fast *(adj.)* **1.** QUICK, RAPID, swift, speedy, fleeting *a fast swimmer* SLOW **2.** SUDDEN, INSTANT *a fast reaction*

fast *(adv.)* **1.** rapidly, swiftly, speedily, quickly *Walk fast.* **2.** suddenly, instantly *happen fast* **3.** tightly *Hold fast to the rope.*

fasten *(v.)* **1.** TIE, hook, clasp, ATTACH, JOIN, SECURE, FIX, bind *Fasten the pin to the blouse.* **unfasten, undo 2.** CONCENTRATE, FOCUS, direct, train *Fasten your mind on the lesson.*

fat *(adj.)* plump, CHUBBY, chunky, portly, stocky, stout, HUSKY, burly, obese, corpulent, rotund **SKINNY, THIN**

fatal *(adj.)* DEADLY, lethal, murderous, ruinous, disastrous **life-giving, beneficial**

fatigue *(n.)* weariness, exhaustion, drowsiness, ENERGY, vitality

fault *(n.)* **1.** DEFECT, blemish, flaw *Repair the fault in the plumbing.* **2.** ERROR, MISTAKE, blame, guilt, offense *It's not my fault.*

favor *(n.)* **1.** KINDNESS, deed, benefit, HELP, SUPPORT *Will you do me a favor?* **2.** regard, admiration, esteem, RESPECT *The principal held the student in good favor.* **disfavor**

favor *(v.)* PREFER, APPROVE

favorite *(adj.)* preferred, DEAR, pet, esteemed, beloved, adored, cherished
the apple of one's eye

• Guess the Idiom •

clue: favorite

answer: the apple of one's eye

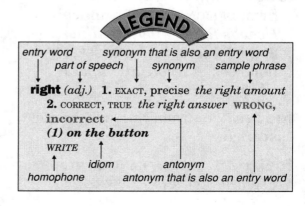

LEGEND

| entry word | synonym that is also an entry word |
| part of speech | synonym | sample phrase |

right *(adj.)* **1.** EXACT, precise *the right amount* **2.** CORRECT, TRUE *the right answer* WRONG, incorrect ←
(1) on the button
WRITE

homophone | idiom | antonym | antonym that is also an entry word

fear (n.) **1.** FRIGHT, dismay, terror, HORROR, ALARM, panic, apprehension *control one's fear* **fearlessness**, COURAGE **2.** phobia, distaste, DREAD, aversion *He has a fear of the dark.*
(1) cold feet

• Guess the Idiom •

clue: fear

answer: cold feet

fearless (adj.) BRAVE, BOLD, DARING, courageous, intrepid, undaunted COWARDLY, **chicken**

fee (n.) **1.** CHARGE, BILL, toll, fare, payment *He paid a fee to enter the zoo.* **2.** REWARD, compensation *She charged a fee to paint the house.*

feeble (adj.) **1.** WEAK, frail, infirm, DELICATE, sickly, unhealthy *He was feeble after his illness.* **2.** ineffective, futile, USELESS, hopeless *A feeble attempt is likely to fail.*

feed (v.) nourish, nurture, nurse **starve**

feel (v.) **1.** TOUCH, HANDLE, grope *Feel the softness.* **2.** SENSE, perceive, UNDERSTAND, EXPERIENCE *Feel the heat.*

feeling (n.) EMOTION, sensation, impression, sentiment

fellow (n.) MAN, chap, guy, MATE, COMPANION, comrade

ferocious (adj.) WILD, fierce, SAVAGE, VIOLENT, BRUTAL, barbarous, bestial GENTLE, TAME, MILD

festival (n.) feast, holiday, celebration, CEREMONY, rite, ritual

feud (n.) QUARREL, argument, dispute, spat, FIGHT, squabble

fight (n.) QUARREL, BATTLE, argument, dispute, clash, conflict, tussle, scuffle, outbreak, fray, BRAWL, RIOT, row, fracas

fight (v.) **1.** QUARREL, DISAGREE, squabble, quibble, FEUD, wrangle, bicker, BATTLE, BOX, STRUGGLE, wrestle, spar, BRAWL *a fight for freedom and equality* **2.** RESIST, COMBAT, oppose, withstand *fight an illness*
(1) take up arms

• Guess the Idiom •

clue: fight

answer: take up arms

figure *(n.)* **1.** FORM, SHAPE, outline, configuration, PATTERN *a beautiful figure* **2.** numeral, digit *Write the figure on the line.* **3.** sum, TOTAL, AMOUNT, PRICE, COST *Calculate the final figures.* **4.** diagram, PICTURE, representation, IMAGE *Refer to Figure A in your math book.*

figure *(v.)* CALCULATE, COUNT, reckon, cipher, TOTAL, appraise, assess

fill *(v.)* **1.** LOAD, PACK, heap, pile, stuff, stock *Fill the truck with supplies.* **2.** SATISFY, fulfill, meet *Fill the requirements of the class.*

filthy *(adj.)* **1.** DIRTY, NASTY, FOUL, squalid, sordid, slovenly, contaminated, polluted *a filthy room* CLEAN **2.** obscene, indecent, foul, DIRTY, vile, sordid, smutty, offensive *filthy language*

final *(adj.)* LAST, latest, conclusive, closing, ultimate, terminal FIRST, **initial**

find *(v.)* LOCATE, DISCOVER, UNCOVER, unearth, EXPOSE, DETECT, ascertain LOSE, **misplace**

fine *(n.)* penalty, punishment, FEE

fine *(adj.)* **1.** EXCELLENT, admirable, select *He did a fine job.* **2.** TINY, minute *fine grains of sand*

finish *(v.)* DO, COMPLETE, accomplish, ACHIEVE, REACH, END, STOP, STAY, CEASE, desist, terminate, arrest BEGIN

fire *(n.)* blaze, flame, flare, GLOW, BURN

firm *(adj.)* **1.** fixed, SET, unchanging, unyielding, definite, STEADY, steadfast, STABLE *a firm decision* **fluctuating, wavering** **2.** solid, HARD *firm muscles* SOFT

first *(adj.)* **1.** beginning, earliest, leading, FRONT *the first chapter of the book* LAST **2.** ORIGINAL, initial, novel, NEW, primary *the first Thanksgiving*

fit *(n.)* outburst, tantrum, seizure

fit *(adj.)* **1.** APPROPRIATE, suitable, pertinent, relevant *a house fit for a king* **2.** HEALTHY *feeling fit*

fix *(v.)* **1.** MEND, REPAIR, PATCH *Let's fix the car.* **2.** restore, IMPROVE, HEAL, CURE, remedy *The doctor will fix the broken bone.* BREAK, DESTROY **3.** FASTEN, ATTACH *Fix the picture to the wall.*

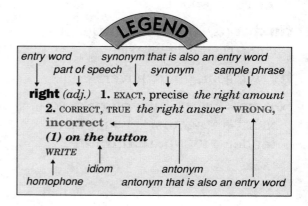

LEGEND

entry word   *synonym that is also an entry word*
  part of speech   *synonym*   *sample phrase*

right *(adj.)* **1.** EXACT, precise *the right amount* **2.** CORRECT, TRUE *the right answer* WRONG, **incorrect**
(1) on the button
WRITE

homophone   *idiom*   *antonym*   *antonym that is also an entry word*

flag *(n.)* pendant, banner

flat *(adj.)* **1.** horizontal, prone, prostrate, recumbent *Lie flat on the ground.* **2.** LEVEL, SMOOTH, even, flush *a flat surface* ROUGH

flatter *(v.)* PRAISE, humor, COMPLIMENT, cajole, laud, extol CRITICIZE
lay it on thick

flavor *(n.)* TASTE, season

flexible *(adj.)* **1.** bendable, supple, pliable, pliant *a flexible hose* RIGID **2.** adaptable, EASY, affable, versatile *a flexible employee*

flimsy *(adj.)* **1.** WEAK, frail, FRAGILE, SHABBY, ramshackle, rickety, DILAPIDATED, SORRY *a flimsy ladder* STRONG **2.** POOR, immaterial, frivolous, trivial, INADEQUATE, worthless *a flimsy argument* substantial **3.** THIN, SHEER, LIGHT *a flimsy fabric* THICK

fling *(v.)* THROW, CAST, TOSS, PITCH, hurl, sling, heave

floor *(n.)* ground, deck, STORY

flow *(v.)* stream, RUN, gush, surge, cascade, spout

fluster *(v.)* CONFUSE, rattle, disconcert, baffle, startle

fly *(v.)* soar, glide, hover

foe *(n.)* ENEMY, adversary, OPPONENT, antagonist, RIVAL, contender FRIEND, teammate

follow *(v.)* **1.** pursue, track, trail, CHASE, HUNT *Follow the criminal's trail.* **2.** SUCCEED, ensue *A discussion will follow the lecture.* **3.** OBEY, heed, comply, submit, OBSERVE *Follow the rules.* DISOBEY

food *(n.)* fare, rations, provisions, nourishment

fool *(n.)* simpleton, dunce, ninny, nincompoop, blockhead, buffoon, booby, moron, dullard, ignoramus, bore, cretin, imbecile, oaf

fool *(v.)* CHEAT, hoax, DECEIVE, dupe, delude
pull the wool over one's eyes

foolish *(adj.)* SILLY, STUPID, RIDICULOUS, senseless, idiotic, ABSURD, unreasonable, shallow, daft, fatuous, frivolous, trifling, imprudent, inept WISE, sensible

forbid *(v.)* BAN, prohibit, disallow, hinder, DENY, REFUSE, veto, taboo ALLOW, PERMIT

force *(v.)* DRIVE, URGE, compel, coerce, oblige, impel, constrain

foreign *(adj.)* alien, STRANGE, unfamiliar, peculiar, exotic, outlandish native

foreigner *(n.)* STRANGER, alien, outsider, immigrant, newcomer

forget *(v.)* disregard, neglect REMEMBER
draw a blank, slip one's mind

forgive *(v.)* EXCUSE, PARDON, RE-LEASE, OVERLOOK, CLEAR, acquit, absolve BLAME, CHARGE
bury the hatchet, let off the hook

form *(n.)* **1.** FIGURE, SHAPE, structure *a carved form of Benjamin Franklin* **2.** KIND, SORT, METHOD *a form of punishment* **3.** STYLE, MANNER, mode *His tennis game is in good form.*

form *(v.)* MAKE, SHAPE, FIGURE, mold, sculpt, contrive

formal *(adj.)* prim, dignified, precise, solemn, ceremonial **informal, casual**

fortunate *(adj.)* LUCKY, blessed, favorable
on top of the heap

fortune *(n.)* **1.** LUCK, CHANCE, FATE, happenstance, serendipity *It was her good fortune to find her lost puppy.* **misfortune**
2. WEALTH, riches, affluence, opulence *He left his fortune to the children.*
(1) how the ball bounces, how the cookie crumbles

foul *(adj.)* **1.** decayed, stinking, ROTTEN, NASTY, vile, rancid, putrid *foul meat* FRESH
2. stormy, RAINY *foul weather*
FOWL

fraction *(n.)* PART, portion, fragment, PIECE, segment, division
WHOLE

fracture *(n.)* BREAK, CRACK, rupture, cleavage, fissure

fracture *(v.)* BREAK, CRACK, rupture, SPLIT, cleave, shatter

fragile *(adj.)* frail, WEAK, DELICATE, tenuous **STRONG, durable**

free *(v.)* RELEASE, untie, liberate, discharge, extricate **constrain, imprison**

free *(adj.)* **1.** gratis, gratuitous, complimentary *a free sample* **costly** **2.** emancipated, untied, LOOSE, liberated, discharged, unrestricted, unfettered, INDEPENDENT *a free citizen* **imprisoned, incarcerated, bound**
(1) on the house

freedom *(n.)* **1.** LIBERTY, liberation, release, independence, emancipation, autonomy *freedom from slavery* **2.** RIGHT, privilege, LICENSE, authorization *the freedom to make one's own decisions*

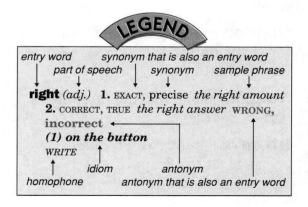

freeze (v.) **1.** CHILL, ice, congeal, numb, refrigerate *Freeze the meat.* **2.** STOP, HESITATE *Freeze in your tracks.*

frequent (v.) hang out, hang around, VISIT, haunt, ATTEND **avoid**

frequent (adj.) **1.** COMMON, OFTEN, customary, everyday, daily *a frequent sight* RARE, **uncommon** **2.** recurrent, repeated, PERSISTENT, numerous *frequent visits to the hospital*

fresh (adj.) **1.** NEW, sweet *fresh bread* OLD, STALE **2.** PURE *fresh air* **3.** vigorous, HEALTHY *fresh from a good night's sleep* **4.** NEW, novel, ORIGINAL, recent *Are there any fresh data from the lab?*

friend (n.) buddy, pal, MATE, chum, COMPANION, partner, comrade, associate, crony ENEMY, FOE, OPPONENT

friendly (adj.) SOCIAL, welcoming, CHEERFUL, personable, hospitable, affable, amicable, congenial UNFRIENDLY, **belligerent**

fright (n.) FEAR, ALARM, TERROR, dismay, PANIC

frighten (v.) SCARE, ALARM, SHOCK, terrify, daunt, THREATEN, menace, intimidate

front (n.) face, facade, fore, anterior BACK

frown (v.) pout, scowl, mope, grieve, SULK, despair SMILE

Go **CRAZY** with **WORDS!**

frighten

MENACE

TERRIFY

FRIGHTEN

frustrate (*v.*) **1.** IRRITATE, BAFFLE, DISCOURAGE, torment, tantalize *Her actions frustrate me.* **2.** BLOCK, foil, thwart, DEFEAT, annul, nullify *The new law frustrated his plans.* ENCOURAGE *(2) take the wind out of one's sails*

fulfill (*v.*) **1.** COMPLETE, FINISH *fulfill the requirements for graduation* **2.** realize, accomplish, ACHIEVE *fulfill a dream* **3.** OBEY, OBSERVE, FOLLOW, MIND, heed, acknowledge, RESPECT *fulfill the letter of the law*

full (*adj.*) **1.** filled, loaded, stuffed *the full glass* EMPTY **2.** COMPLETE, total, WHOLE, ENTIRE *the full story* INCOMPLETE

fun (*n.*) cheer, glee, merriment, amusement, enjoyment, mirth

funny (*adj.*) HUMOROUS, laughable, amusing, entertaining, comical, WITTY, droll, HILARIOUS, farcical, ludicrous, jovial SAD, BORING, DULL

furious (*adj.*) ANGRY, raging, infuriated, fuming, wrathful, irate, frantic CALM, **unruffled**

furnish (*v.*) GIVE, SUPPLY, PROVIDE, EQUIP, outfit, stock

fuss (*n.*) **1.** WORRY, disquiet, unrest *a lot of fuss over what to wear* **2.** ARGUMENT, dispute, QUARREL, squabble *They had a fuss over who was right.*

fuss (*v.*) COMPLAIN, fret, WORRY *make a mountain out of a molehill*

fussy (*adj.*) **1.** fidgety, fretful, RESTLESS, IMPATIENT, cranky *Calm the fussy baby.* **2.** particular, choosy, DIFFICULT, CRITICAL, finicky, discriminating, fastidious *a fussy eater*

Gg

gadget (*n.*) appliance, contraption, INSTRUMENT, DEVICE, TOOL

gain (*v.*) **1.** GET, ACQUIRE, OBTAIN, REACH, attain, EARN, WIN, secure *gain knowledge* **2.** profit, IMPROVE, benefit, ADVANCE *gain understanding from the experience*

gallant (*adj.*) BRAVE, valiant, courageous, heroic, intrepid, noble, chivalrous, courteous, dashing

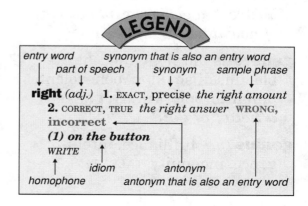

LEGEND

entry word   synonym that is also an entry word
    part of speech   synonym   sample phrase

right (*adj.*) **1.** EXACT, precise *the right amount* **2.** CORRECT, TRUE *the right answer* WRONG, **incorrect**
(1) on the button
WRITE

homophone   idiom   antonym
    antonym that is also an entry word

gamble *(n.)* RISK, CHANCE, speculation, venture
a shot in the dark
GAMBOL

gamble *(v.)* **1.** RISK, BET, wager *gamble at a casino* **2.** speculate *I'll gamble she'll show up at the dance tonight.*
GAMBOL

game *(n.)* **1.** MATCH, CONTEST, COMPETITION, sport, amusement, diversion, recreation *Play the game.* **2.** PREY, quarry *hunting for big game*

gang *(n.)* GROUP, MOB, PACK, crew, BAND, clan, PARTY, herd, clique

garbage *(n.)* TRASH, rubbish, WASTE, litter, REFUSE, JUNK, salvage, debris

gather *(v.)* COLLECT, PICK, ASSEMBLE, accumulate, harvest, reap, muster, garner SCATTER
round up

gaze *(v.)* STARE, gape, regard

general *(adj.)* **1.** COMMON, USUAL, universal, conventional, prevalent, POPULAR *general opinion* **2.** VAGUE, inexact, indefinite, abstract *a general explanation of how it works* **specific**

generous *(adj.)* giving, charitable, unselfish, KIND, benevolent, philanthropic STINGY, CHEAP
a heart of gold

genius *(n.)* brilliance, intelligence, ingenuity, TALENT

gentle *(adj.)* HARMLESS, MILD, docile, INNOCENT, innocuous, inoffensive VIOLENT, ROUGH

genuine *(adj.)* **1.** authentic, REAL, actual, valid, guaranteed *a genuine diamond* **imitation,** FAKE **2.** SINCERE, heartfelt, natural, HONEST *genuine concern*

get *(v.)* **1.** fetch, procure, net, GAIN, annex, requisition *Go and get the tickets.* GIVE, **relinquish** **2.** RECEIVE, ACQUIRE, OBTAIN, EARN, CLEAR, attain, accomplish *We need to get a computer.* LOSE

ghastly *(adj.)* **1.** HORRIBLE, frightening, hideous, grisly, horrendous *a ghastly accident* **2.** shocking, unforgivable, odious, appalling *a ghastly deed that hurt me*

ghost *(n.)* SPIRIT, phantom, specter, vision, spook, apparition

giant *(n.)* MONSTER, behemoth, ogre, colossus

giant *(adj.)* HUGE, ENORMOUS, GIGANTIC, VAST, monstrous, gargantuan, colossal TINY, SMALL

gift *(n.)* **1.** PRESENT, PRIZE, AWARD *a birthday gift* **2.** DONATION, gratuity, offering, blessing, legacy, bequest *a generous gift of money* **3.** talent, SKILL, ABILITY, aptitude *She was born with a gift for music.*

gigantic *(adj.)* GIANT, HUGE, ENORMOUS, IMMENSE, jumbo, colossal, staggering, king-size SMALL, TINY, **minute**

give *(v.)* **1.** grant, PRESENT, donate, CONTRIBUTE, DISTRIBUTE, endow, bestow, confer, allot, allocate *Give her my skates.* TAKE, RECEIVE **2.** SUPPLY, PROVIDE, FURNISH *give advice* GET **3.** BUDGE, MOVE *The door would not give.*

glad *(adj.)* HAPPY, pleased, contented, delighted, CHEERFUL, tickled, elated, jubilant UNHAPPY

gloom *(n.)* **1.** sadness, depression, melancholy, SORROW, woe, doldrums, grief *the gloom caused by separation* **2.** darkness, SHADE, shadow, dusk, murkiness *the gloom of a rainy day*

gloomy *(adj.)* **1.** DARK, dusky, shadowy, DIM, DINGY *a gloomy day* **2.** cheerless, UNHAPPY, depressed, SAD, GLUM, DISMAL, melancholy *a gloomy mood*

glory *(n.)* FAME, HONOR, renown, repute

glow *(v.)* SHINE, gleam, glimmer, blaze

glum *(adj.)* GLOOMY, sullen, MOODY, grumpy, dejected, pessimistic

go *(v.)* ADVANCE, MOVE, CONTINUE, LEAVE, TRAVEL, DEPART, proceed, PASS, progress, BUDGE, STIR STAY, COME, ARRIVE, REMAIN
beat it

goal *(n.)* AIM, PURPOSE, objective, target, intent, intention, OBJECT, END, DESTINATION

good *(adj.)* **1.** SATISFACTORY, ADEQUATE, alright, acceptable *The shoes are a good fit.* **2.** MORAL, upright, virtuous, PLEASANT *a good person* BAD **3.** CORRECT, fitting, APPROPRIATE, JUST, valid, SOUND, USEFUL *a good answer*

gorgeous *(adj.)* BEAUTIFUL, ATTRACTIVE, ravishing, dazzling, radiant, impressive, MAGNIFICENT, resplendent UGLY

gossip *(n.)* hearsay, RUMOR, chatter, tattle, scandal

govern *(v.)* LEAD, RULE, reign, CONTROL, MANAGE, COMMAND, oversee
be in the driver's seat

grab *(v.)* seize, clutch, grasp, CATCH, clasp, clench, CAPTURE, snatch

graceful *(adj.)* ELEGANT, tasteful, FINE, refined, cultured, polished, suave, mannerly AWKWARD

grade *(n.)* **1.** CLASS, CATEGORY, DEGREE *a fine grade of meat* **2.** MARK *a good grade on a test* **3.** SLOPE, gradient, incline *an uphill grade*

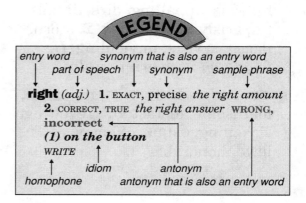

gradual *(adj.)* SLOW, continuous *at a snail's pace*

grand *(adj.)* stately, ROYAL, MAJESTIC, MAGNIFICENT HUMBLE

grateful *(adj.)* THANKFUL, indebted, APPRECIATIVE **ungrateful**

grave *(n.)* vault, crypt, tomb, sepulcher, catacomb

grave *(adj.)* **1.** solemn, SOBER, staid, sedate *a grave occasion* **2.** SERIOUS, IMPORTANT, weighty, CRITICAL *a grave piece of evidence in court* UNIMPORTANT

great *(adj.)* **1.** LARGE, tremendous *a great monument* LITTLE, SMALL **2.** NOBLE, exalted, mighty, notable, distinguished, eminent *a great leader* GRATE

greedy *(adj.)* SELFISH, avaricious, rapacious, covetous GENEROUS

greet *(v.)* MEET, WELCOME, address, salute, hail

grief *(n.)* SORROW, woe, sadness, anguish, MISERY, heartache, AGONY, REGRET, DISTRESS

grim *(adj.)* **1.** HORRIBLE, AWFUL, hideous, appalling, dire, dreadful, grisly *a grim task* **2.** stern, HARSH, SEVERE, unyielding *He fought on with grim resolve.*

gross *(adj.)* DISGUSTING, repulsive, loathsome, distasteful, revolting, sickening, CRUDE, offensive, FOUL, lewd honorable

ground *(n.)* land, PLOT, field, meadow, tract

group *(n.)* **1.** BUNCH, SET, bundle, bale, cluster, COLLECTION, store, PILE *a group of stamps* **2.** PARTY, assembly, association, organization, society, club, COMMITTEE, congregation, forum, clan, clique, RING, league, gathering, CROWD, COMPANY, squad, TEAM, BAND, tribe, FAMILY *a group of people*

grow *(v.)* **1.** mature, DEVELOP, evolve, flourish *grow to adulthood* **2.** cultivate, PRODUCE, RAISE *grow crops*

growth *(n.)* INCREASE, enlargement, development, maturation, expansion, extension

grumpy *(adj.)* MOODY, sullen, GLUM, GLOOMY, temperamental, churlish, PESSIMISTIC CHEERFUL

guard *(v.)* PROTECT, WATCH, shield, DEFEND, SUPPORT

guess *(n.)* conjecture, supposition, ESTIMATE

guess *(v.)* ESTIMATE, surmise, PREDICT, RECKON *take a shot at*

guest *(n.)* visitor, caller, COMPANY

guide *(n.)* LEADER, director, pilot, escort

guide *(v.)* **1.** LEAD, DIRECT, pilot, CONDUCT, STEER, SHOW *guide an expedition* mislead **2.** administer, supervise *The teacher guides the students.* *(1) hold the reins*

guilty *(adj.)* **1.** RESPONSIBLE, culpable, blameworthy *a guilty criminal* INNOCENT **2.** SORRY, remorseful, regretful, contrite, penitent, repentant *a guilty feeling about not helping*

gun *(n.)* weapon, firearm, pistol, rifle, revolver, carbine, musket

gyp *(v.)* CHEAT, mislead, TRICK, DECEIVE, bamboozle, swindle, dupe

Hh

• •

habit *(n.)* CUSTOM, practice, mannerism, tradition, routine, trait, idiosyncrasy

halt *(v.)* **1.** STOP, CEASE, PAUSE *halt at the border* **proceed** **2.** ARREST, curb, terminate, END, quell *halt the abuse*

handle *(v.)* TOUCH, FEEL, grasp

handsome *(adj.)* good-looking, ATTRACTIVE, becoming UGLY

handy *(adj.)* skillful, CLEVER, dexterous, adroit CLUMSY

hang *(v.)* **1.** suspend, dangle, sling *Hang up your coat.* **2.** ATTACH, hook, tack *Hang the picture on the wall.* **3.** hover, float *The clouds hang over the shore.*

happen *(v.)* arise, occur, befall, ensue, DEVELOP, transpire

happiness *(n.)* JOY, enjoyment, merriment, mirth, bliss, contentment, rapture **sadness**

happy *(adj.)* **1.** CHEERFUL, GLAD, joyous, MERRY, festive, light-hearted, delighted, jolly, jubilant, ecstatic *He's in a happy mood.* UNHAPPY, SAD, **downcast, mournful, sorrowful** **2.** contented, satisfied *She's happy with the travel plans.* **dissatisfied**
(1) walking on air

◆ Guess the Idiom ◆

clue: happy

• •
answer: walking on air

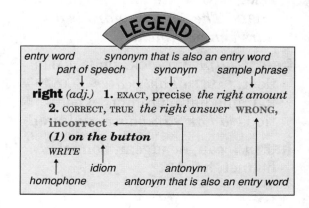

LEGEND

entry word | *synonym that is also an entry word*
part of speech | *synonym* | *sample phrase*

right *(adj.)* **1.** EXACT, precise *the right amount* **2.** CORRECT, TRUE *the right answer* WRONG, **incorrect** ←
(1) on the button
WRITE
idiom *antonym*
homophone *antonym that is also an entry word*

hard *(adj.)* **1.** FIRM, solid, RIGID *a hard surface* SOFT, **limp** **2.** DIFFICULT, COMPLICATED, COMPLEX, tangled, rigorous, INTENSE, intricate, laborious, arduous, irksome *a hard problem to solve* EASY, SIMPLE **3.** insensitive, unfeeling, callous, severe, stern, HARSH *a hard coach* SENSITIVE, GENTLE, KIND

harm *(n.)* injury, DAMAGE, wrong, wickedness, maltreatment

harm *(v.)* **1.** DAMAGE, sabotage, vandalize *harm the relief supplies* **2.** HURT, INJURE, maltreat, impair, ABUSE, victimize *harm the child*

harmful *(adj.)* DANGEROUS, hurtful, ruinous, destructive, injurious HARMLESS, HELPFUL, **beneficial**

harmless *(adj.)* INNOCENT, unoffending, unobjectionable, inoffensive HARMFUL, **hurtful**

harsh *(adj.)* **1.** abrupt, blunt, stern, SEVERE, RUDE, discourteous, unmannerly, gruff, churlish *a harsh voice* **2.** desolate, stark, BARE, barren, RUGGED, BLEAK, EMPTY *The Arctic tundra is a harsh environment.*

hasty *(adj.)* **1.** QUICK, swift, RAPID, fleet, FAST *a hasty eater* SLOW **2.** immediate, prompt, expeditious *a hasty response* **delayed**

hat *(n.)* cap, headgear, bonnet, helmet, hood

hate *(n.)* malice, rancor, SPITE, resentment, enmity, antagonism LOVE

hate *(v.)* DISLIKE, DESPISE, scorn, spurn, disdain, detest, loathe, abhor, abominate LOVE

hazard *(n.)* DANGER, peril, jeopardy, threat, CHANCE, RISK

heal *(v.)* CURE, restore, revive, IMPROVE, FIX, remedy, recover

healthy *(adj.)* WELL, SOUND, robust, hearty, vigorous ILL

hear *(v.)* LISTEN, heed, ATTEND, harken, regard
learn through the grapevine

◆ **Guess the Idiom** ◆

clue: hear

answer: learn through the grapevine

heavy *(adj.)* **1.** weighty, bulky, hefty, unwieldy, cumbersome *The weights are too heavy to lift.* LIGHT **2.** DIFFICULT, troublesome, imposing, oppressive, overwhelming, burdensome *The news is heavy.*

help *(n.)* AID, assistance, RELIEF, SUPPORT **hindrance**

help *(v.)* AID, ASSIST, SERVE, SUPPORT, relieve, benefit, abet, ally, COOPERATE **hinder, obstruct, oppose**
lend a hand, pitch in

helper *(n.)* COMPANION, ally, assistant, partner, colleague

helpful *(adj.)* **1.** USEFUL, beneficial, practical, pragmatic, utilitarian *a helpful tool* USELESS **2.** FRIENDLY, neighborly, KIND, benevolent, philanthropic *a helpful neighbor* **unfriendly**

helpless *(adj.)* **1.** WEAK, dependent *A newborn baby is helpless.* INDEPENDENT **2.** powerless, unarmed, vulnerable, unprotected, unguarded *The town was helpless during the storm.* **guarded,** SAFE

hero *(n.)* CHAMPION, victor, winner, idol

hesitate *(v.)* PAUSE, DELAY, waver, DOUBT, demur
drag one's feet

hidden *(adj.)* concealed, covered, masked, unexplained, obscure CONSPICUOUS, **visible**

hide *(v.)* COVER, CONCEAL, screen, mask, BURY, obscure, DISGUISE DISCOVER, **reveal, disclose, unmask**

high *(adj.)* **1.** TALL, lofty, elevated *a high mountain* LOW **2.** shrill,

SHARP, piercing, acute, piping *a high scream* LOW

hilarious *(adj.)* FUNNY, comical, MERRY, mirthful, jolly, jocund

hill *(n.)* SLOPE, incline, SLANT, mound, knoll, gradient

hint *(n.)* SIGN, tip, CLUE, indication, inkling, suggestion
a bug in one's ear

◆ Guess the Idiom ◆

clue: hint

....

answer: a bug in one's ear

hint *(v.)* SUGGEST, MENTION, imply, insinuate, intimate, allude, prompt

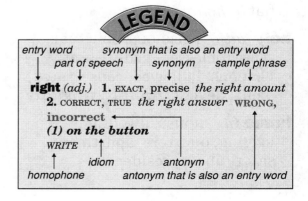

hire *(v.)* USE, EMPLOY, engage, CONTRACT, enlist **fire**

hit *(v.)* STRIKE, assault, BEAT, WHIP, lash, thrash, flog, ram, pound, whack, smack, collide, smite

hobo *(n.)* tramp, loafer, vagrant, beggar, outcast, vagabond

hold *(v.)* **1.** grip, grasp, clutch, clasp, KEEP, BEAR, CARRY, cradle, possess *Hold the camera in your hand.* **2.** CONTAIN, STORE, accommodate *What does the box hold?* **3.** KEEP, SAVE, STAY, retain, reserve, arrest *Hold back your anger.* **4.** convene, ORGANIZE *hold a meeting*

hole *(n.)* **1.** pit, WELL, hollow, burrow, lair, cavity *The squirrel dug a hole in the ground.* **2.** opening, outlet, aperture, perforation, void *a hole in the wall* WHOLE

hollow *(adj.)* **1.** EMPTY, unfilled, excavated, concave, indented, vacant *a hollow tree* **2.** FALSE, INSINCERE, hypocritical, deceptive *hollow promises* **3.** USELESS, fruitless, profitless, worthless *hollow actions* **4.** muffled, DULL, flat *a hollow sound*

holy *(adj.)* RELIGIOUS, spiritual, sacred, blessed, godly, saintly, virtuous, hallowed, consecrated, pious, devout **unholy, ungodly**

home *(n.)* HOUSE, dwelling, lodging, quarters, apartment, SPACE, abode, residence

honest *(adj.)* truthful, trustworthy, GENUINE, FAIR, MORAL, upright, frank, righteous, reliable, dependable, respectable, honorable, JUST, GOOD, virtuous, diligent, conscientious, scrupulous, reputable DISHONEST, **deceitful, unfair**
above board

honesty *(n.)* TRUTH, sincerity, frankness, veracity **deception**

honor *(n.)* integrity, virtue, principle, esteem, regard, admiration, RESPECT, rectitude
a feather in one's cap

◆ **Guess the Idiom** ◆

clue: honor

answer: a feather in one's cap

honor *(v.)* RESPECT, esteem, regard, venerate DISGRACE

hop *(v.)* JUMP, LEAP, SPRING, vault, bound

hope *(n.)* WISH, DESIRE, longing, anticipation, aspiration

hope *(v.)* WISH, EXPECT, DESIRE, anticipate
look on the sunny side

horrible *(adj.)* TERRIBLE, AWFUL, dreadful, dire WONDERFUL, TERRIFIC

horrid *(adj.)* frightful, ghastly, alarming, horrifying, hideous, dreadful, gruesome

horror *(n.)* TERROR, FEAR, FRIGHT, DREAD, awe, panic, ALARM

horse *(n.)* steed, charger, mount, nag, pony, stallion, mare, gelding, foal, filly, colt, yearling, equine *HOARSE*

hostile *(adj.)* **1.** antagonistic, contrary, adverse, opposed, aggressive, warlike, belligerent *Two hostile countries fought a war.* **2.** UNFRIENDLY, unkind, COLD, MEAN, malicious, malevolent *a hostile look* KIND, **hospitable,** FRIENDLY

hot *(adj.)* **1.** WARM, burning, scorching, blazing, fiery, torrid, sweltering, sizzling *hot to the touch* COLD, **icy 2.** SPICY, biting, pungent, piquant *a hot chili pepper* BLAND, MILD

Go CRAZY with WORDS!

hot

house (*n.*) HOME, SHELTER, dwelling, apartment, SPACE, lodging, residence, quarters, abode

hug (*v.*) **1.** caress, embrace, snuggle, coddle, CLING, enfold *hug a child* **2.** near, APPROACH *The boats hug the shore.*

huge (*adj.*) tremendous, GIGANTIC, ENORMOUS, VAST, IMMENSE, monstrous, colossal, massive

humble (*adj.*) modest, unassuming, unpretentious **arrogant**

humiliate (*v.*) SHAME, EMBARRASS, mortify, degrade, humble

humorous (*adj.*) FUNNY, amusing, WITTY, comical, laughable, RIDICULOUS SERIOUS, **solemn**

hungry (*adj.*) starving, famished, ravenous FULL, **satiated**

hunt (*n.*) quest, pursuit

hunt (*v.*) pursue, SEARCH, SEEK, stalk, CHASE, FOLLOW, track

hurry (*v.*) **1.** RUSH, hasten, quicken, SPEED, accelerate, RACE, SCURRY, PRESS, hustle *hurry to work* DELAY, **dawdle**, LINGER **2.** expedite, precipitate *You cannot hurry the vote count.* SLOW, **prolong**
(1) shake a leg, race against the clock

hurt (*v.*) **1.** INJURE, cripple, wound, BRUISE, mistreat, ABUSE, HARM, disable, maim, mutilate, disfigure *Did you hurt your hand in a fall?* **2.** ACHE, sting, throb, smart *His broken leg hurts.*

husky (*adj.*) **1.** hoarse, grating, rough, HARSH *a husky voice* **2.** STURDY, RUGGED *The man had a husky build.*

hustle (*v.*) **1.** HURRY, RUSH, SPEED, hasten, scurry, DASH *Hustle down the street.* **2.** prompt, URGE, goad, accelerate, pressure, compel, FORCE, coerce *Hustle everyone into the room.*

hut (*n.*) shed, shack, shanty, CABIN, hovel

hysterical (*adj.*) **1.** HILARIOUS, sidesplitting *a hysterical laugh* **2.** MAD, crazed, excitable, raving, frantic, WILD, berserk *hysterical behavior*

Ii

idea (*n.*) **1.** THOUGHT, notion, belief, CONCEPT, OPINION, fancy, PLAN, theory, VIEW, supposition, conception, perception, inspiration, impression *a good idea for a show* **2.** topic, theme, SUBJECT *the main idea of the story*

ideal (*adj.*) perfect, faultless, exemplary **average, normal, typical**

identical (*adj.*) SAME, ALIKE, indistinguishable, DUPLICATE, twin **dissimilar, DIFFERENT, distinctive**

identify (*v.*) **1.** RECOGNIZE, distinguish, discern *identify the lost child* **2.** relate, CONNECT, ally *identify with her feelings*
(2) walk in another's shoes, see through another's eyes

idiot (*n.*) FOOL, dunce, clod, oaf, dolt, buffoon, jester

idle (*adj.*) **1.** LAZY, inactive, sluggish, indolent, dawdling, slothful *an idle person* **industrious, diligent, hardworking, active** **2.** unoccupied, vacant, EMPTY *After the family moved, their house stood idle.* BUSY **3.** FOOLISH, vain, UNNECESSARY, unproductive, ineffective, ineffectual *He made an idle attempt to stop the horse as it ran by.*
IDOL

idol (*n.*) **1.** deity, god, IMAGE, STATUE, icon, effigy *worship a false idol* **2.** favorite, HERO, heroine, star, celebrity *a teenage idol*
IDLE

ignite (*v.*) LIGHT, BURN, inflame, kindle **extinguish**

ignorant (*adj.*) uneducated, illiterate, unaware, unconscious, uninformed **educated, knowing, AWARE**
in the dark

ignore (*v.*) disregard, neglect, OVERLOOK, snub, slight, OMIT, DEFY, RESIST, REJECT **COMPREHEND, REALIZE, RECOGNIZE**
bury one's head in the sand

◆ Guess the Idiom ◆

clue: ignore

answer: bury one's head in the sand

ill (*adj.*) **1.** SICK, sickly, ailing, unhealthy, unsound, indisposed, unwell *care for the ill child* **WELL, HEALTHY** **2.** BAD, EVIL, WICKED, WRONG, CORRUPT *ill intentions* **GOOD, respectable**
(1) under the weather

illegal (*adj.*) unlawful, forbidden, criminal, unconstitutional **LEGAL, authorized**
under the table

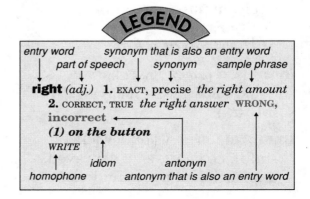

LEGEND

entry word   synonym that is also an entry word
   part of speech   synonym   sample phrase

right (*adj.*) **1.** EXACT, precise *the right amount* **2.** CORRECT, TRUE *the right answer* WRONG, **incorrect**
(1) on the button
WRITE

homophone   idiom   antonym   antonym that is also an entry word

illusion *(n.)* vision, hallucination, mirage, delusion

illustrate *(v.)* **1.** DRAW, PICTURE, portray, depict *illustrate the flowers* **2.** DEMONSTRATE, SHOW, EXPLAIN, elucidate *illustrate how the heart works*

image *(n.)* **1.** likeness, representation, reproduction, FORM *the spitting image of one's mother* **2.** CONCEPT, IDEA, THOUGHT, notion, fancy *the image of a world without hunger*

imaginary *(adj.)* unreal, illusory, supposed, fanciful, visionary REAL, ORDINARY, SIMPLE

imagine *(v.)* THINK, fancy, picture, suppose, conceive, presume, ASSUME, envisage, surmise

imitate *(v.)* COPY, DUPLICATE, REPRODUCE, FOLLOW, mimic, mock, REFLECT, mirror, parody, ape

immaculate *(adj.)* spotless, stainless, CLEAN, NEAT, TIDY DIRTY, FILTHY

immediately *(adv.)* promptly, instantaneously, STRAIGHTAWAY, directly, spontaneously, instinctively, impulsively **slowly, deliberately** *at the drop of a hat*

immense *(adj.)* VAST, ENORMOUS, HUGE, colossal SMALL, TINY, **minute**

immoral *(adj.)* WRONG, WICKED, sinful, CORRUPT, BAD, depraved, unprincipled, unscrupulous, warped, perverted MORAL, **righteous**

immortal *(adj.)* eternal, undying, ENDLESS **mortal, perishable**

immune *(adj.)* protected, invulnerable, inoculated, SAFE **vulnerable, susceptible**

impatient *(adj.)* **1.** uneasy, ANXIOUS, RESTLESS, jittery *feeling impatient before the big game* **tolerant, lenient** **2.** testy, IRRITABLE, fretful, SHORT, RUDE, brusque, hotheaded *impatient because of one's headache* **3.** EAGER, keen, excited *impatient to get the project started* **unhurried**

impolite *(adj.)* RUDE, discourteous, boorish, brash, insolent, inconsiderate, tactless POLITE, COURTEOUS

important *(adj.)* **1.** NECESSARY, ESSENTIAL, weighty, GRAVE, vital, significant, staple, momentous, SERIOUS, monumental, urgent, imperative, pressing *an important announcement* **insignificant** **2.** FAMOUS, VALUABLE *an important government official*

impossible *(adj.)* unattainable, inconceivable, unworkable, unimaginable, hopeless, ABSURD POSSIBLE, LIKELY, **probable** *out of one's reach*

impostor *(n.)* impersonator, pretender, quack, phony, charlatan *wolf in sheep's clothing*

improper *(adj.)* inappropriate, indiscreet, tactless

improve *(v.)* ENHANCE, BETTER, ADVANCE, CORRECT, FIX, rectify, reform

inaccurate *(adj.)* incorrect, WRONG, inexact, imprecise, unsound ACCURATE, CORRECT, **precise**
off base, full of hot air

inadequate *(adj.)* insufficient, unsatisfactory, deficient, lacking ADEQUATE, **sufficient**, ENOUGH

incapable *(adj.)* **1.** incompetent, unable, unqualified, inept *incapable of doing a good job* **competent, skilled 2.** powerless, impotent, HELPLESS, defenseless, WEAK *incapable of defending oneself* POWERFUL
(1) not cutting the mustard

incident *(n.)* EVENT, occurrence, occasion, happening, proceeding, experience

include *(v.)* **1.** INVOLVE *include in the game* EXCLUDE **2.** CONTAIN, ENCLOSE, comprise, embrace *What does the packet include?*

income *(n.)* wages, revenue, proceeds

incomplete *(adj.)* **1.** partial, unfinished *an incomplete story* COMPLETE, **finished 2.** deficient, lacking, defective, wanting *an incomplete thought* **thorough, conclusive**

inconvenient *(adj.)* AWKWARD, untimely, inopportune, cumbersome, annoying CONVENIENT, **suitable**, HANDY

increase *(v.)* GAIN, GROW, ENLARGE, MAGNIFY, amplify, RISE, mount, MULTIPLY, EXPAND, STRETCH, ADVANCE, EXTEND DECREASE, LESSEN, REDUCE, DROP

incredible *(adj.)* **1.** unbelievable, unrealistic, improbable, fictitious, suspect, doubtful, preposterous *an incredible lie*
2. FANTASTIC, WONDERFUL, MARVELOUS, EXTRAORDINARY *an incredible trip to Greece*

independent *(adj.)* **1.** FREE, self-reliant, unrestricted, free-thinking *an independent person*
2. self-governing, autonomous *an independent country*

inexpensive *(adj.)* CHEAP, low-priced, reasonable, economical, budget EXPENSIVE, **costly**

infect *(v.)* CONTAMINATE, taint, pollute, CORRUPT, AFFECT **disinfect**

inferior *(adj.)* **1.** BAD, AWFUL, POOR, shoddy, RANK *an inferior job* **superior, supreme 2.** MINOR, insignificant, UNIMPORTANT *an inferior work of art* MAJOR, **higher**

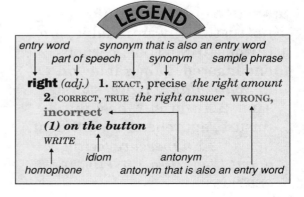

LEGEND

entry word — *synonym that is also an entry word*
part of speech — *synonym* — *sample phrase*

right *(adj.)* **1.** EXACT, precise *the right amount*
2. CORRECT, TRUE *the right answer* WRONG, **incorrect** ←
(1) on the button
WRITE
homophone — *idiom* — *antonym* — *antonym that is also an entry word*

influence (*n.*) **1.** POWER, force, potency, STRENGTH, WEIGHT, CONTROL, leadership, guidance, DIRECTION *his influence on the presidential race* **2.** importance, prestige, standing *reach a level of influence in the community*

influence (*v.*) **1.** CONTROL, DIRECT, GOVERN, MANAGE, LEAD, GUIDE *influence the crowd* **2.** AFFECT, sway, modify, CHANGE, alter, transform *influence the outcome of the game*

inform (*v.*) TELL, ADVISE, notify, relate, apprise, brief

information (*n.*) facts, data, KNOWLEDGE, news, tidings

inhabit (*v.*) occupy, reside, abide, DWELL, SETTLE, LOCATE

injure (*v.*) HURT, WRONG, BRUISE, sprain, strain, wrench, DAMAGE, impair, ABUSE, maltreat

innocent (*adj.*) guiltless, HARMLESS, naive, ingenuous, unaffected GUILTY
wet behind the ears

inquire (*v.*) ASK, QUESTION, query, quiz, INVESTIGATE, interrogate

insecure (*adj.*) **1.** unsafe, untrustworthy, unreliable, precarious, DANGEROUS, perilous, endangered, vulnerable *an insecure hiding place* SECURE, SAFE **2.** TIMID, SHY, hesitant, unsure, apprehensive, diffident, NERVOUS *an insecure feeling about the future* CONFIDENT, CERTAIN

insincere (*adj.*) DISHONEST, deceitful, underhanded, hypocritical SINCERE, HONEST
full of bologna

• Guess the Idiom •

clue: insincere

answer: full of bologna

insist (*v.*) DEMAND, STRESS, PRESS, pressure, compel, prompt
put one's foot down

• Guess the Idiom •

clue: insist

answer: put one's foot down

inspect (*v.*) EXAMINE, STUDY, evaluate, VIEW, REVIEW, survey, scrutinize, peruse, appraise

inspire (v.) **1.** ENCOURAGE, enliven, stimulate, invigorate *The coach must inspire the players.* **2.** inhale, BREATHE, gasp *inspire two deep breaths* **3.** prompt, instigate, incite *inspire a change in one's attitude*

instant (n.) moment, second, flash, jiffy

instant (adj.) immediate, SUDDEN, abrupt, instantaneous, expeditious
in the twinkling of an eye

instinct (n.) **1.** intuition, impulse, inclination, leaning *follow one's instinct* **2.** TALENT, GIFT, ABILITY, aptitude, flair, knack *a natural instinct for fixing things*

instruct (v.) TEACH, tutor, INFORM, TRAIN, EDUCATE, enlighten

instrument (n.) **1.** DEVICE, TOOL, implement, utensil, GADGET *a medical instrument* **2.** means, WAY, mover, catalyst *an instrument of destruction*

insult (v.) OFFEND, ABUSE, RIDICULE, HUMILIATE, jeer, mock, taunt, snub, outrage, affront COMPLIMENT, FLATTER
fling dirt at

intelligent (adj.) BRIGHT, QUICK, CLEVER, ALERT, quick-witted, knowing STUPID, IGNORANT

intend (v.) MEAN, signify, propose, PLAN, contemplate

intense (adj.) **1.** SEVERE, extreme, acute, HARSH, cutting *intense pain* **2.** EAGER, EARNEST, ENTHUSIASTIC, ardent, fervent, zealous, passionate *an intense fan*

interest (n.) **1.** attention, regard, engagement, consideration *an interest in the arts* **2.** SHARE, PART, portion, PIECE *buy an interest in the company* **3.** benefit, profit, advantage *an interest in the property deal*

interest (v.) **1.** ATTRACT, engage, engross, ABSORB, captivate, mesmerize *interest the audience* **2.** CONCERN, INVOLVE, AFFECT *Her problems do not interest me.*
(1) catch one's eye

interesting (adj.) absorbing, fascinating, entertaining, amusing, compelling BORING, DULL, **uninteresting**

interfere (v.) **1.** meddle, intervene, INTRUDE *interfere in their relationship* **2.** obstruct, hamper, BLOCK, FRUSTRATE *interfere with getting one's job done*
(1) put one's two cents in

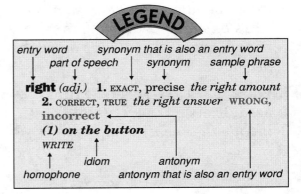

71

interrupt (v.) **1.** STOP, suspend, discontinue, sever, DISCONNECT, DISTURB, hinder *interrupt progress* **2.** INTERFERE, INTRUDE *interrupt with an emergency call*

introduce (v.) **1.** PRESENT, acquaint *introduce someone to your parents* **2.** START, ANNOUNCE, commence, initiate, precipitate *introduce the program* CONCLUDE **3.** insert, interject *introduce harmful substances into the air*
(1) give the floor to

> ◆ **Guess the Idiom** ◆

clue: introduce

answer: give the floor to

intrude (v.) **1.** trespass, INTERFERE, meddle *intrude in someone else's business* **2.** INVADE, infringe, encroach *intrude on one's privacy*

invade (v.) **1.** ATTACK, overrun, assault, RAID, STORM, assail *invade the enemy camp*

2. INTRUDE, INTERRUPT, intervene *invade the private meeting*

invent (v.) originate, CREATE, conceive, concoct, devise

investigate (v.) RESEARCH, EXPLORE, EXAMINE, INSPECT, scrutinize, STUDY, probe

invisible (adj.) HIDDEN, concealed, indiscernible, imperceptible VISIBLE, OBVIOUS

invite (v.) **1.** REQUEST, ASK, beckon, summon *invite to a party* **2.** ATTRACT, entice, TEMPT, LURE *invite trouble*
(2) leave the door open

involve (v.) **1.** CONCERN, AFFECT *a situation that does not involve you* **2.** INCLUDE, CONTAIN, comprise *What does the job involve?* **3.** ABSORB, engage, preoccupy, commit *involve oneself in one's work*

irritable (adj.) testy, peevish, touchy, GRUMPY, cranky, grouchy, cantankerous, IMPATIENT, crabby, MOODY

irritate (v.) **1.** chafe, inflame *irritate the skin* **2.** provoke, ANNOY, BOTHER, pester, exasperate, ruffle, DISTURB, needle *irritate one's teacher*
(2) tread on one's toes, get one's goat

item (n.) article, DETAIL, feature, component, ingredient

Jj

∙ ∙

jail *(n.)* prison, lockup, dungeon

jail *(v.)* confine, imprison, commit, incarcerate FREE, RELEASE

jam *(v.)* **1.** crowd, SQUEEZE, ram, wedge, sandwich, CRAM *jam clothes into the suitcase* **2.** obstruct, BLOCK, plug, hinder *jam the exit door*

jar *(n.)* bottle, urn, vase, crock, pot, jug, flask

jealous *(adj.)* resentful, envious, covetous
green with envy

jerk *(n.)* IDIOT, FOOL, moron, booby, simpleton, clod, nerd, numskull, goof

jerk *(v.)* jolt, PULL, twitch, SHAKE

job *(n.)* WORK, occupation, employment, profession, craft, calling, vocation

join *(v.)* **1.** UNITE, COMBINE, ATTACH, CONNECT, merge, cement, splice, graft, link, couple, adhere *join the pieces together* SEPARATE, DISCONNECT **2.** ally, associate *join the club* QUIT, RESIGN

joke *(n.)* gag, jest, TRICK, hoax, prank, deception, antic

journey *(n.)* TRIP, VOYAGE, venture, expedition, jaunt, excursion, passage

joy *(n.)* DELIGHT, HAPPINESS, pleasure, CHEER, excitement, bliss, rapture, elation, felicity grief, dejection, pessimism

judge *(n.)* referee, umpire, arbitrator

judge *(v.)* CONSIDER, regard, scrutinize, sentence, CONDEMN

judgment *(n.)* intelligence, discrimination, tact, discernment, diplomacy, understanding

jump *(v.)* **1.** HOP, LEAP, SPRING, vault, SKIP, bound *Jump over the log.* **2.** DIVE, plunge *The diver jumped off the platform.* **3.** startle, flinch, START *She jumped in surprise.*

jungle *(n.)* thicket, forest, bush

junk *(n.)* SCRAP, TRASH, salvage, rubbish, GARBAGE, WASTE, litter, debris, REFUSE

just *(adj.)* **1.** RIGHT, FAIR, lawful, legitimate, justified, reasonable, impartial *a just decision* **2.** deserved, earned, DUE, APPROPRIATE *one's just punishment*

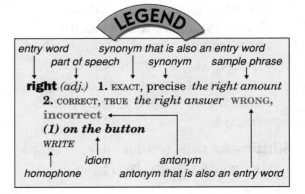

LEGEND

entry word   synonym that is also an entry word
    part of speech   synonym   sample phrase
right *(adj.)* **1.** EXACT, precise *the right amount* **2.** CORRECT, TRUE *the right answer* WRONG, incorrect
(1) on the button
WRITE
        idiom   antonym
homophone   antonym that is also an entry word

justice *(n.)* fairness, impartiality, legitimacy

justify *(v.)* **1.** DEFEND, FORGIVE, absolve, exonerate, acquit *justify one's actions* **2.** SUPPORT, warrant, authorize, legitimize, substantiate *information that would justify his decision to quit*

Kk

●●●●●●●●●●●●●●●●●●●●●

keep *(v.)* **1.** SAVE, HOLD, SECURE, reserve, PRESERVE, CONSERVE *keep the doll* DISCARD, REJECT **2.** MAINTAIN, tend, PROTECT, GUARD *keep the lawn mowed* **3.** detain, retain, confine *keep from escaping* RELEASE

kill *(v.)* execute, MURDER, slay, slaughter, butcher, smother, annihilate, exterminate, massacre, assassinate SPARE

kind *(n.)* GROUP, SORT, TYPE, CLASS, species

kind *(adj.)* FRIENDLY, loving, NICE, COURTEOUS, CONSIDERATE, HELPFUL, PLEASANT, sympathetic, compassionate, affectionate, THOUGHTFUL, TENDER, WARM, liberal, cordial, DEVOTED, EARNEST, humane, charitable, ardent, benevolent MEAN, UNFRIENDLY, HOSTILE

kindness *(n.)* tenderness, sympathy, compassion **brutality**

king *(n.)* RULER, sovereign, monarch, majesty

kingdom *(n.)* realm, province, REGION, domain

kiss *(n.)* smooch, embrace

kit *(n.)* tools, EQUIPMENT, outfit, COLLECTION

knife *(n.)* dagger, blade, dirk, stiletto, SWORD, saber, cutlass, rapier, scimitar

knock *(v.)* tap, rap, HIT, STRIKE, bang, thump

know *(v.)* UNDERSTAND, COMPREHEND, perceive, RECOGNIZE, discriminate, fathom, gather, surmise *get the picture* NO

knowledge *(n.)* learning, understanding, WISDOM, JUDGMENT, INFORMATION, intelligence **ignorance**

Ll

●●●●●●●●●●●●●●●●●●●●●

labor *(n.)* **1.** WORK, employment, JOB, occupation, living, livelihood, chore, ERRAND, DUTY *earn the fruits of one's labor* **2.** WORKERS, employees, hands *We'll hire extra labor to finish the job.*

labor *(v.)* WORK, toil

lack *(n.)* WANT, NEED, shortage, shortcoming, sparsity, scarcity, dearth, void

lack *(v.)* NEED, REQUIRE, MISS

language *(n.)* SPEECH, dialect, tongue

large *(adj.)* BIG, BROAD, VAST, extensive, roomy, spacious, HUGE, IMMENSE, ENORMOUS, GIANT, GIGANTIC, colossal SMALL, **miniature**

last *(v.)* CONTINUE, STAY, REMAIN, endure, persist, abide

last *(adj.)* **1.** FINAL, latter, hindmost, terminal, closing, ultimate *the last act of the play* FIRST, **foremost 2.** recent, latest *the last time you went to the movies*

late *(adj.)* tardy, behind, delayed, slack EARLY, **ahead**

laugh *(v.)* giggle, titter, snigger, cackle, chuckle, guffaw, snicker CRY, **lament**
crack up, roll in the aisles

law *(n.)* RULE, regulation, ORDER, mandate, standard, principle, doctrine, statute, decree, tenet, ordinance, edict

lay *(v.)* **1.** PUT, place, SET, rest, deposit, plant, park *lay the book on the table* **2.** ASSIGN, attribute, ascribe *lay blame* **3.** MAKE, devise, PREPARE *lay a plan*

lazy *(adj.)* IDLE, sluggish, inactive, passive, lifeless, slack, indolent, slothful **industrious,** ACTIVE, ALERT, EAGER

Go CRAZY with WORDS!

large

75

lead (*v.*) **1.** COMMAND, GOVERN, RULE, CONTROL *lead the army* **2.** GUIDE, DIRECT, pilot, STEER *lead the way* FOLLOW **call the shots, be in the driver's seat**

leader (*n.*) BOSS, CHIEF, head, director, manager, GUIDE, principal **follower**

leak (*v.*) trickle, seep, ooze, drip, dribble

lean (*v.*) **1.** incline, SLANT, tilt, SLOPE, bank *lean to the left* **2.** DEPEND, rely *lean on for support*

lean (*adj.*) **1.** THIN, gaunt, SLIM, SKINNY *a lean figure* FAT **2.** nonfat *lean meat* **3.** POOR, deficient, nonproductive *lean years* **productive, teeming**

leap (*v.*) JUMP, SPRING, bound, vault, HOP

learn (*v.*) master, MEMORIZE, DISCOVER, ACQUIRE, grasp, REMEMBER, ascertain

least (*adj.*) smallest, tiniest, feeblest, slightest **most**

leave (*v.*) **1.** DEPART, EXIT, PART, vacate, SCRAP, ABANDON, DESERT, forsake, migrate, emigrate, EVACUATE *leave the area* ARRIVE, REACH, JOIN **2.** QUIT, retire, withdraw, RESIGN *leave one job for another* **3.** will, bequeath, PROMISE *She'll leave her jewelry to her daughter.* **(1) take a powder**

lecture (*n.*) TALK, address, LESSON, discourse, sermon

legend (*n.*) fable, myth, TALE

lend (*v.*) **1.** LOAN, GIVE, ADVANCE *lend one's baseball mitt to one's best friend* **2.** FURNISH, PROVIDE, CONTRIBUTE *lend some help*

lessen (*v.*) DECREASE, REDUCE, SHRINK, condense, compress, CONCENTRATE, diminish, dwindle, deduct, SUBTRACT, ELIMINATE, taper, narrow, wane, ebb, subside, abridge INCREASE, EXPAND, **BUILD** **cut short** *LESSON*

lesson (*n.*) **1.** assignment, exercise, PRACTICE, teaching, recitation *The guitar lesson begins at noon.* **2.** warning, admonition *learn a lesson from stealing* *LESSEN*

let (*v.*) ALLOW, PERMIT, consent, grant, APPROVE FORBID, **prohibit**

level (*v.*) **1.** flatten, equalize *level the ground for planting* **2.** DESTROY, demolish, RAZE *The tornado might level the town.*

level (*adj.*) **1.** FLAT, HORIZONTAL, EVEN, SMOOTH, *skate on a level surface* **2.** EQUAL, balanced *level competition* **3.** CALM, even-tempered, collected, composed, unruffled *a level head*

liberty *(n.)* **1.** FREEDOM, independence, autonomy *They fought for liberty.* **2.** privilege, RIGHT, LICENSE, PERMISSION *the liberty to stand up for one's rights*

license *(n.)* PERMIT, consent, authorization, approval

license *(v.)* PERMIT, ALLOW, consent, authorize, sanction, warrant

lick *(v.)* lap, TASTE, moisten

lie *(n.)* untruth, STORY, falsehood, fib, prevarication, fabrication

lie *(v.)* **1.** recline, REST, lounge, repose *lie on the couch* **2.** fib, slander, defame, prevaricate *lie to her mother*
(2) break one's word, stretch the truth

life *(n.)* **1.** being, existence, ENERGY, SPIRIT, viability *lose one's life in a car accident* **2.** NATURE, creation *protect all of life*

lift *(v.)* **1.** RAISE, BOOST, hoist, ELEVATE, SUPPORT *lift the box* **lower** **2.** IMPROVE, BOOST, promote, exalt *lift one's spirits* **depress** **3.** END, revoke *lift the blockade*

light *(v.)* **1.** brighten, illuminate, illumine *The flashlight will light our way.* **2.** IGNITE, BURN, kindle, fire *Light the fire.*

light *(adj.)* **1.** PALE, white, wan, FAINT, pallid *a light complexion* DARK, **black, dim** **2.** portable, movable, buoyant *light enough to carry* HEAVY

like *(v.)* ADMIRE, VALUE, APPRECIATE, APPROVE, prize, ENJOY, RESPECT, PREFER, esteem, relish DISLIKE, HATE, **loathe**
get a kick out of, stuck on

likely *(adj.)* probable, POSSIBLE, apt, promising

limit *(n.)* boundary, BORDER, perimeter

limit *(v.)* **1.** bound, confine, restrict, curb, prohibit, STAY *limit progress* **2.** determine, specify, fix, demarcate *limit the area that can be used*
(2) clip one's wings

linger *(v.)* WAIT, STAY, REMAIN, loiter, DELAY, tarry, dawdle, procrastinate, lollygag, loaf DEPART, **vacate**

list *(n.)* register, ROLL, index, catalog

list *(v.)* RECORD, register, chronicle, catalog, index

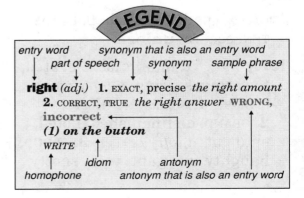

77

listen *(v.)* **1.** HEAR, harken, ATTEND *listen to the speech* **2.** OBEY, MIND, heed *listen to your mother's advice*
(1) lend an ear

little *(adj.)* SMALL, TINY, minute, miniature, slight, petite, wee, microscopic, puny BIG, HUGE, **colossal**

live *(v.)* **1.** STAY, DWELL, INHABIT, occupy, REMAIN *live in a white house* **2.** EXIST, survive, be, abide, endure, subsist, persist *live for eighty years* DIE

lively *(adj.)* ACTIVE, nimble, spirited, brisk, QUICK, agile, spry DULL, **sluggish**

load *(n.)* CARGO, freight, burden, shipment

loan *(n.)* ADVANCE, credit

loan *(v.)* LEND, ADVANCE, credit

locate *(v.)* **1.** PLACE, FIX *locate the house far from the road* **2.** FIND, DISCOVER, UNCOVER, unearth *locate the missing keys* **3.** SETTLE, occupy *locate in a different state*
(2) put one's fingers on
(3) hang up one's hat

lock *(v.)* padlock, latch, bolt, FASTEN, secure **unlock**

lofty *(adj.)* **1.** HIGH, TALL, elevated, towering, soaring *a lofty mountain* LOW, SHORT, **sunken** **2.** GRAND, distinguished, noted, eminent *a lofty career* **3.** PROUD, haughty, arrogant, vain, snotty, snobbish *lofty ideals* MODEST
(3) on one's high horse

lonely *(adj.)* lone, ALONE, solitary, apart, SEPARATE, desolate

long *(v.)* DESIRE, WANT, pine, hanker
set one's heart on

long *(adj.)* lengthy, protracted, extended, outstretched

look *(v.)* **1.** glance, glimpse, peep, peer, STARE, gape, GAZE, WATCH, regard *look at the bird* **2.** EXAMINE, INSPECT, INVESTIGATE, scrutinize *look it over* **3.** SEARCH, SEEK, HUNT *look for your notebook* **4.** APPEAR, SEEM *look good in blue*
(1) have your eye on

loose *(adj.)* hanging, limp, slack TIGHT

lose *(v.)* **1.** mislay, misplace *lose your watch* FIND, LOCATE **2.** FAIL, forfeit, relinquish, forgo, sacrifice, YIELD *lose the game* WIN, **triumph**

lost *(adj.)* **1.** missing, disappeared *a lost ship* **2.** forgotten *a lost memory* **3.** hopeless, irreversible, irretrievable *a lost cause* **4.** wasted, squandered, misspent *make up for lost time* **5.** confused, perplexed, baffled *lost by the explanation*

loud *(adj.)* NOISY, blaring, shrill, boisterous, clamorous, rowdy, vociferous, thunderous QUIET, SOFT, STILL

love (*n.*) affection, adoration, fondness, devotion

love (*v.*) ADMIRE, ADORE, WORSHIP, HONOR, CHERISH, esteem, revere HATE, DESPISE
think the world of

lovely (*adj.*) **1.** BEAUTIFUL, ATTRACTIVE *a lovely girl* **2.** delightful, INTERESTING *a lovely song* **3.** MAGNIFICENT, scenic *a lovely view*

low (*adj.*) **1.** sunken, unelevated *low land* HIGH, **elevated** **2.** SHORT *a low ceiling* **3.** shallow, reduced, diminished, decreased, lessened *low tide, low funds* **4.** FEEBLE, WEAK, FRAGILE, DELICATE, sickly *in low health* **5.** SAD, depressed, dejected, dispirited *in a low mood*

loyal (*adj.*) FAITHFUL, TRUE, DEVOTED, CONSTANT, unchanging, STABLE, PERMANENT, staunch **disloyal, traitorous**

loyalty (*n.*) devotion, allegiance

luck (*n.*) FATE, RISK, CHANCE, FORTUNE, happenstance, serendipity, prosperity, FAVOR, SUCCESS

lure (*v.*) ATTRACT, entice, decoy, TEMPT

luxury (*n.*) splendor, opulence, abundance

luxurious (*adj.*) RICH, plush, extravagant, lavish, SPLENDID, opulent

Mm

machine (*n.*) appliance, DEVICE, TOOL, implement

mad (*adj.*) **1.** CROSS, ANGRY, fretful, testy, IRRITABLE, annoyed, cranky, grouchy, exasperated, ornery, disgruntled, enraged, petulant, peevish *mad at a friend* **2.** CRAZY, insane *The man was mad.* SANE, **rational**

magic (*n.*) **1.** sorcery, wizardry, incantation, voodoo, conjury, hocus-pocus *an act of magic* **2.** SPELL, INFLUENCE, charm, trance *under one's magic*

magical (*adj.*) enchanting, CHARMING, fascinating, entrancing, mystical, incantational

magnificent (*adj.*) **1.** GRAND, SPLENDID, resplendent, glorious *a magnificent palace* **2.** NOBLE, MAJESTIC, imposing, stately, regal *a magnificent leader*

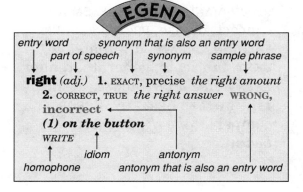

magnify (v.) **1.** ENLARGE, amplify, INCREASE *Magnify the size of the object.* REDUCE **2.** EXAGGERATE, overstate *magnify the truth* **understate 3.** intensify, heighten, STRENGTHEN, AGGRAVATE, worsen *magnify the problem* **de-escalate**

maid (n.) attendant, servant, domestic, HELP, employee *MADE*

main (adj.) MAJOR, foremost, CHIEF, principal, primary, leading, IMPORTANT, essential *MANE*

maintain (v.) **1.** SUPPORT, KEEP, sustain, PRESERVE, nurse *maintain the garden* **2.** DECLARE, assert, profess *maintain his innocence* **3.** CONTINUE, persist, persevere *maintain one's course*

majestic (adj.) regal, ROYAL, stately, SPLENDID, MAGNIFICENT

major (adj.) **1.** CHIEF, IMPORTANT, primary, principal *a major piece of evidence* **2.** greater, larger, higher, utmost *a major influence*

make (v.) **1.** BUILD, CONSTRUCT, erect, MANUFACTURE, ASSEMBLE, concoct, devise, PRODUCE, FORM, FASHION, CREATE, originate, INVENT, fabricate, generate, render *Let's make a birdhouse.* **demolish, WRECK, DESTROY 2.** FORCE, compel *Make the dog well-behaved.*

manage (v.) **1.** HANDLE, manipulate, wield *manage the controls* **2.** supervise, administer, GUIDE, CONDUCT, superintend *manage the team*

manner (n.) **1.** METHOD, mode, FASHION, WAY, STYLE *a manner of speaking* **2.** behavior, aspect, APPEARANCE *a polite manner* *MANOR*

manor (n.) estate, mansion *MANNER*

manufacture (v.) MAKE, PRODUCE, CONSTRUCT, BUILD, fabricate

many (adj.) numerous, PLENTIFUL, countless, various, bountiful, innumerable, abundant, profuse **few, infrequent, scant**

march (v.) **1.** WALK, STEP, pace, parade *march in the parade* **2.** ADVANCE, proceed *march on an enemy*

mark (n.) **1.** STAIN, smudge, notch, score, trace, smear *erase the mark* **2.** stamp, brand, seal, imprint, endorsement *the king's mark*

marry (v.) wed, espouse, betroth, unite, JOIN *tie the knot* *MERRY*

marvelous (adj.) WONDERFUL, amazing, astonishing, wondrous, EXTRAORDINARY, exceptional, AWFUL, HORRIBLE

match (n.) GAME, CONTEST, COMPETITION, trial

mate (n.) **1.** FRIEND, associate, COMPANION *a good mate* **2.** spouse, wife, husband, partner *Choose a mate.*

mate (v.) MARRY, match, breed

material (n.) **1.** MATTER, substance, STUFF *an unknown material* **2.** fabric, textile *She bought material to make a dress.*

matter (n.) **1.** substance, MATERIAL, MEDIUM *The three forms of matter are solid, liquid, and gas.* **2.** difficulty, TROUBLE, DISTRESS, ailment, WORRY, PROBLEM, predicament, dilemma, quandary *What's the matter?*

mature (adj.) adult, grown, grown-up, ripe **immature, YOUNG**

maybe (adv.) perhaps, possibly, perchance, conceivably **surely, certainly**

meal (n.) feast, banquet, spread, snack, repast

mean (v.) indicate, signify, denote, imply, INTEND, EXPRESS

mean (adj.) unkind, CRUEL, heartless, bad-tempered, aggressive, EVIL, merciless, beastly, HOSTILE, SAVAGE, fierce, ruthless, atrocious, despicable, antagonistic, malicious **KIND, GENTLE, sympathetic, FRIENDLY**

meaning (n.) **1.** significance, SENSE, essence, explanation, gist *The meaning is clear.* **2.** PURPOSE, AIM, OBJECT, import, intention, design *the meaning of his actions*

measure (n.) SIZE, gauge, rule, extent, dimension

measure (v.) rule, gauge, appraise, ESTIMATE

medicine (n.) DRUG, ointment, potion, lozenge, PILL, tablet, antidote, salve

medium (adj.) middle, mean, AVERAGE, mediocre

meet (v.) **1.** ASSEMBLE, congregate, convene, muster *The club will meet on Monday.* **2.** ENCOUNTER, GREET, address, WELCOME, converge *Meet me at the corner later today.* **(2) run across** MEAT

melt (v.) thaw, defrost, liquefy, DISSOLVE **harden, jell, FREEZE**

memorize (v.) REMEMBER, NOTE, commit FORGET *learn by heart*

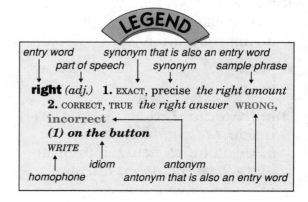

memory *(n.)* **1.** recollection, remembrance, retention, RECALL *lose one's memory in the accident* **2.** SOUVENIR, memento, token *He kept the coin as a memory of his trip.*

mention *(v.)* DECLARE, TELL, STATE

mercy *(n.)* PITY, pardon, forgiveness, compassion, charity, sympathy, clemency

merry *(adj.)* HAPPY, CHEERFUL, sprightly, blithe, jolly, jovial **somber,** SOBER, GLOOMY, SAD

mess *(n.)* **1.** CLUTTER, disorder, disarray, chaos *clean up the mess* **2.** PROBLEM, jam, plight, difficulty, confusion, muddle, predicament, mayhem, snafu *in a real mess*

message *(n.)* dispatch, communication, letter, NOTE, news, tidings

messenger *(n.)* carrier, courier, envoy

messy *(adj.)* untidy, disordered, DIRTY, jumbled, muddled, disheveled CLEAN, TIDY, **neat, orderly**

method *(n.)* system, technique, WAY, COURSE, mode, MANNER, means, operation

middle *(n.)* CENTER, CORE, interior, heart

middle *(adj.)* **1.** central, interior, inside *the middle house on the block* EDGE **2.** neutral, intermediate *to stand on middle ground in an argument*

might *(n.)* POWER, STRENGTH, force, potency

mild *(adj.)* GENTLE, meek, TENDER, placid, BLAND, nonabrasive **stormy,** VIOLENT, SPICY

mimic *(adj.)* IMITATE, mime, COPY, copycat, ape, mock

mind *(n.)* intellect, intelligence

mind *(v.)* **1.** regard, MARK, monitor *Mind your manners.* **disregard** **2.** OBEY, heed *Mind your mother.* DISOBEY, DEFY **3.** GUARD, WATCH, PROTECT, ATTEND *Mind the store while I'm away.* **(3) keep an eye on**

◆ **Guess the Idiom** ◆

clue: mind

answer: keep an eye on

---

minor *(n.)* child, YOUTH

minor *(adj.)* smaller, lesser, INFERIOR, UNIMPORTANT, insignificant, petty, trite MAJOR, **significant**

miracle *(n.)* marvel, WONDER, prodigy, phenomenon, SIGN, omen

mischief *(n.)* **1.** naughtiness, roguery, prankishness *involved in mischief* **2.** HARM, injury, DAMAGE *repair the mischief*

miserable *(adj.)* **1.** UNHAPPY, wretched, forlorn, distressed *a miserable mood* HAPPY, **elated** **2.** POOR, worthless, valueless *miserable living conditions*

misery *(n.)* DISTRESS, anguish, heartache, woe, unhappiness, suffering, GRIEF, SORROW DELIGHT, JOY, **rapture**

miss *(v.)* **1.** SKIP, OMIT, disregard, IGNORE, blunder *miss an opportunity* **2.** WANT, yearn *miss your best friend*
(1) **go in one ear and out the other**

⬩ Guess the Idiom ⬩

clue: miss

answer: go in one ear and out the other

mistake *(n.)* ERROR, SLIP, BLUNDER, oversight, offense, failing, ACCIDENT, FAULT, BUNGLE

mix *(n.)* mixture, VARIETY, medley, hodgepodge, BLEND, composite

mix *(v.)* mingle, COMBINE, merge, JOIN, BLEND, scramble, churn, agitate

mob *(n.)* CROWD, horde, throng

modern *(adj.)* recent, LATE, NEW, novel, FRESH, present **old-fashioned, outmoded,** ANCIENT

modest *(adj.)* HUMBLE, PLAIN, SIMPLE, unpretentious, bashful meek, reserved **boastful, arrogant,** PROUD

money *(n.)* currency, coins, FEE, wages, compensation, salary, cash, funds, WEALTH, riches

monster *(n.)* demon, fiend, VILLAIN, ogre, brute, colossus

mood *(n.)* humor, NATURE, TEMPER, temperament, disposition, SPIRIT, vein

moody *(adj.)* CROSS, sullen, sulky, GLOOMY, dismal, somber, morose CHEERFUL, **good-natured,** HAPPY

moral *(adj.)* GOOD, JUST, virtuous, upright, HONEST IMMORAL, DISHONEST, BAD

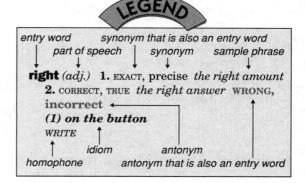

LEGEND

entry word   synonym that is also an entry word
   part of speech   synonym   sample phrase

right *(adj.)* **1.** EXACT, precise *the right amount* **2.** CORRECT, TRUE *the right answer* WRONG, **incorrect**
(1) **on the button**
WRITE

homophone   idiom   antonym   antonym that is also an entry word

morning *(n.)* sunrise, dawn, day-break

motion *(n.)* **1.** movement, action, gesture *a hand motion* **2.** proposal, suggestion *make a motion before student council*

move *(v.)* GO, proceed, pass, advance, continue, shift, march, stir, BUDGE, depart, travel, relocate STAY, REMAIN

multiply *(v.)* **1.** INCREASE, GAIN, GROW, augment *The problems may multiply.* DECREASE **2.** reproduce, breed, procreate, propagate *Rabbits multiply quickly.*

mumble *(v.)* mutter, murmur, slur
swallow one's words

clue: mumble

answer: swallow one's words

murder *(n.)* slaying, killing, homicide, massacre, execution, assassination, carnage

murder *(v.)* KILL, slay, butcher, massacre, execute, assassinate, exterminate, slaughter

mystery *(n.)* SECRET, PUZZLE, RIDDLE, QUESTION, PROBLEM, dilemma, predicament, enigma

Nn

name *(n.)* label, term, title, head, heading, designation, caption

name *(v.)* **1.** label, term, entitle *Name the child.* **2.** MENTION, LIST, designate, cite *Name the winners.*

nap *(v.)* SLEEP, snooze, DOZE, slumber
catch forty winks

narrow *(adj.)* slender, THIN, SLIM, CLOSE, tight, confined WIDE, BROAD, **roomy**

nasty *(adj.)* **1.** DIRTY, FILTHY, FOUL, unclean, polluted, contaminated *nasty water* **2.** disagreeable, unpleasant, distasteful, OBNOXIOUS *a nasty disposition*

nature *(n.)* **1.** QUALITY, CHARACTERISTIC *Explain the nature of the problem.* **2.** personality, MOOD, disposition, temperament *a pleasant nature*

naughty *(adj.)* mischievous, disobedient, unruly, defiant, noncompliant, BAD GOOD, OBEDIENT

near *(adj.)* CLOSE, NEXT, adjacent, neighboring, immediate, proximate, adjoining FAR, **remote, distant**

neat *(adj.)* TIDY, CLEAN, spotless, orderly, uncluttered, spruce, STRAIGHT, SMART **untidy, cluttered,** DIRTY

necessary *(adj.)* required, essential, unavoidable, indispensable, obligatory UNNECESSARY, **needless**

need *(n.)* necessity, requirement, demand, LACK, urgency, requisite, exigency

need *(v.)* REQUIRE, LACK, WANT *KNEAD*

nervous *(adj.)* ANXIOUS, worried, disturbed, RESTLESS, jittery, uneasy, TENSE, concerned, apprehensive CALM, **relaxed** *on pins and needles*

new *(adj.)* **1.** unused, FRESH, untouched, recent, mint *a shiny new penny* OLD, ANCIENT, STALE **2.** novel, MODERN, LATE, latest, innovative, pioneering, unprecedented *a new computer* **old-fashioned, outmoded** *GNU, KNEW*

next *(adj.)* impending, approaching, forthcoming, CLOSE, imminent

nice *(adj.)* **1.** COURTEOUS, FRIENDLY, KIND, WARM, PLEASANT, affable, amiable, cordial *a nice salesclerk* **offensive,** MEAN, UNFRIENDLY **2.** MILD, sunny, WARM, PLEASANT *a nice day*

noble *(adj.)* dignified, upright, stately, ROYAL, MAJESTIC, regal, lordly, aristocratic, imperial, GALLANT, VALIANT, chivalrous **ignoble,** COMMON, **barbaric**

noise *(n.)* SOUND, signal, tone, hubbub, bustle, RACKET, ruckus, flurry, commotion, uproar, disturbance, din, clamor, tumult, turmoil, upheaval QUIET, **stillness, silence**

◆ Guess the Idiom ◆

clue: nervous

answer: on pins and needles

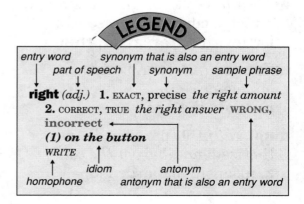

LEGEND

entry word	synonym that is also an entry word

part of speech | synonym | sample phrase

right *(adj.)* **1.** EXACT, precise *the right amount* **2.** CORRECT, TRUE *the right answer* WRONG, **incorrect** ←

(1) on the button
WRITE

homophone | idiom | antonym | antonym that is also an entry word

noisy *(adj.)* LOUD, rowdy, disorderly, boisterous, vociferous, clamorous QUIET, **silent**

nonsense *(n.)* gibberish, drivel, twaddle, rubbish, balderdash, folly, absurdity SENSE

normal *(adj.)* natural, ORDINARY, REGULAR, established, USUAL, typical, standard, COMMON, commonplace, legitimate, customary UNUSUAL, **irregular, unnatural, uncommon, abnormal,** ODD

nosy *(adj.)* CURIOUS, inquisitive, prying

note *(n.)* **1.** NOTICE, memo, memorandum, RECORD, COMMENT, LETTER *Write a note.* **2.** tone *Sing a high note.*

note *(v.)* **1.** NOTICE, OBSERVE, heed, ATTEND *Note the date.* **2.** jot, WRITE, RECORD, inscribe *Note when the assignment is due.*

notice *(n.)* NOTE, poster, SIGN, advertisement, ad, flyer

notice *(v.)* SEE, perceive, regard, OBSERVE, heed, discern MISS, OVERLOOK, IGNORE

now *(adv.)* IMMEDIATELY, instantly, directly, currently, presently, forthwith **later, after, then**

nuisance *(n.)* PEST, BOTHER, annoyance ***pain in the neck***

numb *(adj.)* **1.** paralyzed, anesthetized *numb from the cold* **2.** insensitive, hardened, unemotional, apathetic, dispassionate, unfeeling *numb from the experience of war* **feeling,** SENSITIVE

number *(n.)* **1.** digit, numeral, AMOUNT, FIGURE *Read the number.* **2.** TOTAL, COUNT, QUANTITY *What number of guests will attend?*

Oo

• •

obedient *(adj.)* compliant, submissive, respectful, subservient **disobedient,** NAUGHTY

obey *(v.)* heed, YIELD, KEEP, submit, comply DISOBEY, **DEFY, RESIST**

object *(n.)* **1.** THING, article, FACT *Examine the rare object.* **2.** AIM, GOAL, objective, target, PURPOSE *the object of the meeting*

object *(v.)* oppose, REFUSE, protest, DISAPPROVE, spurn **AGREE**

obnoxious *(adj.)* offensive, repulsive, unpleasant, disagreeable, odious

observe *(v.)* **1.** NOTICE, SEE, behold, DETECT, discern, MIND *Observe the parade.* OVERLOOK **2.** HONOR, RECOGNIZE, commemorate *Observe the holiday.*

obtain *(v.)* GET, ACQUIRE, procure, GAIN, SECURE **LOSE**

obvious *(adj.)* evident, CLEAR, visible, definite, observable, distinct, marked HIDDEN, **obscure**

odd *(adj.)* UNUSUAL, abnormal, QUEER, irregular, atypical, WEIRD, UNIQUE, peculiar, eccentric, quirky USUAL, **typical**, ORDINARY

offend *(v.)* UPSET, IRRITATE, vex, ANNOY, trespass, transgress, sin, displease, disgust, outrage *step on the toes of*

offer *(n.)* bid, proposal, suggestion, proposition refusal, denial

offer *(v.)* GIVE, bestow, PRESENT, propose, bid, tender, submit, SURRENDER, proffer REFUSE, DENY

often *(adv.)* frequently, repeatedly, regularly **never, rarely**

okay *(n.)* approval, authorization

okay *(adj.)* **1.** reasonable, SOUND, sensible, acceptable, JUST, rational *an okay decision* **2.** satisfied, alright, CONTENT *feel okay*

old *(adj.)* **1.** aged, elderly, senior, mature, grown-up, adult *an old person* YOUNG **2.** STALE *old bread* FRESH **3.** ANCIENT, antique, obsolete *old relics* NEW *(1) over the hill*

omit *(v.)* MISS, disregard, neglect, IGNORE INCLUDE

open *(v.)* unfasten, undo, untie, unlock, unseal CLOSE, SHUT

open *(adj.)* **1.** unlocked, unsealed, uncovered, ajar *an open door* SHUT, CLOSED **2.** HONEST, SINCERE, frank, candid *an open conversation* **guarded**

operate *(v.)* **1.** MANAGE, WORK, USE, DIRECT, PERFORM *The farmer operated the bulldozer.* **2.** cut, open up *operate on a patient*

opinion *(n.)* VIEW, viewpoint, IDEA, belief, impression, perspective

opponent *(n.)* RIVAL, competitor, adversary, ENEMY, FOE, antagonist **ally**, FRIEND, **associate, accomplice, protagonist**

opposite *(adj.)* contrary, unlike, adverse, opposed, dissimilar, contradictory SAME, **similar**

order *(n.)* **1.** sequence, arrangement *alphabetical order* **2.** COMMAND, demand, DIRECTION, RULE, regulation *give an order*

order *(v.)* **1.** sequence, ARRANGE, SORT, classify, categorize, file, systematize *order according to last name* **2.** COMMAND, DIRECT, DEMAND, INSIST, prescribe *Order the children to line up.* **3.** REQUEST, commission *order dinner*

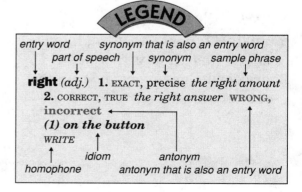

LEGEND

entry word   synonym that is also an entry word
   part of speech   synonym   sample phrase

right *(adj.)* **1.** EXACT, precise *the right amount* **2.** CORRECT, TRUE *the right answer* WRONG, incorrect
(1) on the button
WRITE

homophone   idiom   antonym   antonym that is also an entry word

ordinary *(adj.)* COMMON, REGULAR, USUAL, universal UNIQUE, SPECIAL

organize *(v.)* ARRANGE, PLAN, ORDER, CONSTRUCT **disorganize**

original *(adj.)* **1.** creative, novel, FRESH, NEW *an original design* **2.** FIRST, primary, initial *the original cast of the play*

outrageous *(adj.)* **1.** FANTASTIC, unconventional *outrageous clothes* **logical, sensible** **2.** excessive, extreme, immodest, immoderate *an outrageous amount of money* MODEST, **conservative**

outstanding *(adj.)* **1.** EXCELLENT, GREAT, SUPERB, TERRIFIC, smashing, sensational *an outstanding performance* **2.** OBVIOUS, CONSPICUOUS, prominent, notable *an outstanding student* **3.** unpaid, DUE, uncollected, payable *an outstanding debt*

overlook *(v.)* **1.** MISS, disregard, IGNORE, neglect *overlook the clue* **2.** EXCUSE, FORGIVE, PARDON *overlook the mistake*

overthrow *(v.)* BEAT, DESTROY, CONQUER, overpower, subdue, overturn, vanquish

own *(v.)* **1.** possess, HOLD, have *own a dog* **2.** ADMIT, CONFESS, acknowledge, avow *own up to a crime* DENY

Pp

● ●

pack *(n.)* **1.** BAND, GANG, GROUP *a pack of wolves* **2.** package, bundle, parcel *Carry the pack.*

pack *(v.)* load, stuff, STORE, stow, CRAM, compress

pain *(n.)* **1.** ACHE, AGONY, suffering, torture *severe pain* **2.** DISTRESS, MISERY, SORROW, grief, heartache, anguish, torment *the pain of feeling left out*
PANE

pale *(adj.)* DIM, FAINT, wan, pallid, ashen DARK
PAIL

panic *(n.)* FRIGHT, ALARM, TERROR, DREAD, dismay, trepidation, hysteria CALM, **tranquil**

paper *(n.)* **1.** document, RECORD, manuscript, composition, certificate *She wrote a paper about dinosaurs.* **2.** stationery, papyrus, letterhead *Write a letter on nice paper.*

pardon *(v.)* FORGIVE, absolve, excuse, CLEAR, acquit, liberate

part *(n.)* **1.** PIECE, portion, SHARE, slice, division, component, FRACTION, fragment, element, feature, DETAIL, SECTION *a part of the puzzle* WHOLE, **sum** **2.** role, character *a part in a play*

party (*n.*) **1.** affair, EVENT, reception, festivity, spree, fling, celebration, CEREMONY, feast, FESTIVAL *a birthday party*
2. GROUP, gathering, assemblage *How many are in your party?*

pass (*n.*) **1.** ROAD, avenue, WAY *take the pass across the mountain* **2.** gorge, ravine *It was a deep mountain pass.* **3.** PERMIT, LICENSE, NOTE *need a hall pass*

pass (*v.*) **1.** elapse, lapse, CEASE *The time will pass.* **2.** MOVE, proceed, CONTINUE, GO *Pass by the school.* **3.** SEND, DELIVER, hand *Pass the note.* **4.** surpass, EXCEED, excel *The airplane passed the speed of sound.* **5.** DIE, CEASE *When did your uncle pass away?* **6.** APPROVE, enact, LICENSE, PERMIT, ALLOW *Congress passed the bill into law.*

past (*adj.*) former, previous, prior, earlier **present, future**

paste (*v.*) glue, STICK, bind, ATTACH, bond, fuse, secure, cement

patch (*v.*) MEND, REPAIR, FIX, restore

path (*n.*) **1.** trail, track, ROAD, WAY, COURSE, ROUTE, passage *a path through the woods* **2.** orbit, circuit *Earth's path around the sun*

patience (*n.*) tolerance, endurance, perseverance, composure, calmness, aplomb **impatience, excitability**
PATIENTS

patient (*adj.*) understanding, CALM, persevering, PERSISTENT IMPATIENT, **skittish**

pattern (*n.*) model, SAMPLE, prototype, specimen

pause (*n.*) DELAY, REST, interval, respite
PAWS

pause (*v.*) DELAY, REST, HESITATE, WAIT, waver CONTINUE, **proceed, persist**
catch one's breath
PAWS

• Guess the Idiom •

clue: pause

answer: catch one's breath

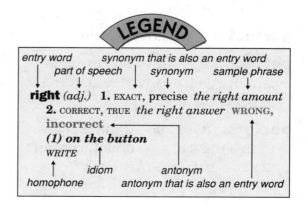

LEGEND

entry word · · · · synonym that is also an entry word
· · part of speech · · synonym · · sample phrase
right (*adj.*) **1.** EXACT, precise *the right amount*
2. CORRECT, TRUE *the right answer* WRONG, incorrect ←
(1) on the button
WRITE
· · · · · idiom · · · · antonym
homophone · · antonym that is also an entry word

89

pay *(n.)* payment, salary, wages, allowance, compensation, remittance, stipend

pay *(v.)* SETTLE, square, discharge, reward, compensate, remit
foot the bill

peace *(n.)* **1.** CALM, QUIET, stillness, respite *peace in the house* **2.** truce, armistice *peace between nations* WAR **3.** EASE, COMFORT, serenity, harmony, concord, solace *peace of mind* **discord, conflict, strife**
PIECE

peaceful *(adj.)* CALM, STILL, settled, tranquil, composed, pacific, placid, serene

peak *(n.)* TOP, summit, apex, acme, pinnacle, zenith BASE, BOTTOM
PEEK

peel *(n.)* rind, SKIN
PEAL

people *(n.)* **1.** humans, persons, folk, individuals *A thousand people participated in the parade.* **2.** PUBLIC, population, society, COMMUNITY, masses, populace *a park for the people*

perfect *(v.)* IMPROVE, refine

perfect *(adj.)* flawless, unblemished, PURE, COMPLETE, ACCURATE **faulty, flawed**

perform *(v.)* **1.** DO, ACHIEVE, execute, FULFILL, ACT, enact, commit, EFFECT *perform the work*

2. ENTERTAIN, function *perform in the play*

perfume *(n.)* aroma, fragrance, SCENT

permanent *(adj.)* **1.** lasting, enduring, perpetual, everlasting, eternal *a permanent home for the puppy* **2.** unchangeable, unalterable, fixed *a permanent tooth*

permission *(n.)* consent, leave, LICENSE, LIBERTY, authorization

permit *(n.)* LICENSE, voucher, warrant, LIBERTY

permit *(v.)* LET, ALLOW, LEAVE, LICENSE, tolerate, grant, APPROVE, sanction, consent, legalize FORBID, BAN, **prohibit**

persistent *(adj.)* CONSTANT, enduring, DETERMINED, STUBBORN, steadfast, relentless

persuade *(v.)* CONVINCE, INFLUENCE, COAX, URGE, entice, induce, **dissuade**
put the pressure on

pest *(n.)* BOTHER, NUISANCE

pick *(v.)* **1.** select, CHOOSE, TAKE, DECIDE, PREFER, cull *pick a movie* **2.** NAME, appoint, designate, nominate, elect *pick a candidate* **3.** GATHER, pluck *pick flowers*
(1) make up one's mind

picture *(n.)* illustration, drawing, diagram, photo, photograph, snapshot, portrait, likeness, IMAGE, PRINT, engraving

piece (n.) BIT, tidbit, SCRAP, PART, crumb, morsel, FRACTION, fragment, SHARE, portion, division, SECTION, remnant
PEACE

pier (n.) dock, jetty, WHARF, landing, quay

pierce (v.) DRILL, puncture, bore, poke, RIDDLE, perforate

pile (n.) heap, mound, mass, store, SUPPLY

pile (v.) COLLECT, GATHER, amass, accumulate, stack

pill (n.) tablet, MEDICINE, capsule, lozenge

pitch (v.) **1.** THROW, CAST, FLING, hurl, toss *pitch a ball* **2.** erect, RAISE *pitch a tent*

pity (n.) compassion, MERCY, sympathy

pity (v.) sympathize, commiserate, condole

place (n.) **1.** location, locality, SPOT, site, POINT, position *a place on the map* **2.** AREA, REGION, district, quarter, territory, tract, ENVIRONMENT, surroundings, habitat *a quiet place to live*

plain (adj.) SIMPLE, unadorned, ORDINARY, natural **decorated, FANCY, ornate**
PLANE

plan (n.) DESIGN, scheme, sketch, chart, draft, program, schedule, COURSE, agenda, tactics, program, procedure, proposal, policy, platform, strategy, stratagem

plan (v.) **1.** ARRANGE, ORGANIZE, schedule, PROGRAM *Let's plan the day's events.* **2.** scheme, anticipate, PLOT, conceive, devise, contrive, concoct, propose, INVENT, IMAGINE *We plan to buy a boat.* **3.** DESIGN, chart, SKETCH, draft *a plan for a three-bedroom house*

play (n.) SHOW, drama, performance

play (v.) **1.** romp, frolic, frisk, sport, gambol, caper *Play outside.* **2.** engage, COMPETE, contend *Next week we play another team.* **3.** OPERATE, WORK *play the piano* **4.** TOY, trifle *play with someone's feelings* **5.** PERFORM, ACT *play a leading role*
(1) horse around

pleasant (adj.) agreeable, delightful, pleasurable, amiable **unpleasant, DISGUSTING**

please (v.) SERVE, gratify, pander, PROVIDE, oblige **displease, OFFEND**

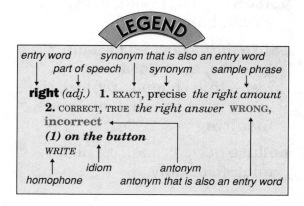

pledge *(n.)* PROMISE, VOW, oath, *covenant*

pledge *(v.)* PROMISE, VOW, guarantee

plentiful *(adj.)* abundant, numerous, RICH, fruitful, FULL, ample, copious, profuse **sparse, SCANT, MEAGER**

plenty *(n.)* ENOUGH, abundance, sufficiency **scarcity**

plot *(n.)* **1.** PLAN, conspiracy, scheme, strategy *a plot to overthrow a government* **2.** theme, ACTION *a plot of a story* **3.** patch, site *a plot of land*

plow *(v.)* WORK, till, cultivate, furrow

poem *(n.)* rhyme, verse, lyric, ballad

point *(n.)* **1.** END, TIP *the point of the pencil* **2.** GOAL, AIM, END, PURPOSE *the point of the discussion*

point *(v.)* SHOW, indicate, gesture, denote, HINT, imply

poison *(n.)* potion, venom, toxin, contaminate, pollutant

poison *(v.)* CONTAMINATE, pollute, INFECT, taint, corrupt

polite *(adj.)* COURTEOUS, KIND, gracious, accommodating, respectful, obliging, refined, civil RUDE, IMPOLITE, **discourteous, insulting**

pollute *(v.)* CONTAMINATE, defile, taint, foul, sully

ponder *(v.)* THINK, WONDER, reflect, CONSIDER, contemplate, meditate, envisage, ruminate, presume

poor *(adj.)* **1.** penniless, needy, destitute, impoverished, HUMBLE, unpretentious *homeless and poor* RICH, **affluent, wealthy 2.** wretched, woeful, pitiable, pathetic, forlorn *a poor neighborhood* GOOD, VALUABLE, FORTUNATE **3.** INFERIOR, unsatisfactory, faulty, sorry *poor telephone service* EXCELLENT, **exceptional,** FINE
(1) in the red (2) down on one's luck
POUR, PORE

pop *(v.)* BURST, EXPLODE, detonate

popular *(adj.)* **1.** FAVORITE, wellliked, FAMOUS, approved, accepted *a popular singer* **unpopular 2.** current, COMMON, prevailing *a popular style of music*

pose *(n.)* posture, POSITION, ATTITUDE, deportment, stance, carriage

pose *(v.)* **1.** model, SIT *pose for a picture* **2.** PRETEND, feign, masquerade *pose as a policeman* **3.** PRESENT, EFFECT, REPRESENT *pose a problem for a debate*

position *(n.)* **1.** PLACE, locality, locale, SPOT *The batter is in position.* **2.** employment, JOB, POST *hired for the position* **3.** STATE, CONDITION, STATION, situation, circumstances *a position of authority* **4.** posture, POSE, ATTITUDE *the position of your body*

positive *(adj.)* **1.** CLEAR, SURE *a positive identification* **negative, doubtful** **2.** CONFIDENT, decided, emphatic, hopeful, optimistic, promising, heartening *a positive feeling about winning the race* **pessimistic, cynical**

possess *(v.)* **1.** OWN, have *possess three cats* **2.** DEMONSTRATE, evidence, manifest *possess great musical talent*

possible *(adj.)* LIKELY, feasible, potential, practicable, achievable IMPOSSIBLE, **inconceivable,** ABSURD
within reach

pour *(v.)* stream, FLOW, RUSH, issue, spout
come down in buckets
POOR

◆ **Guess the Idiom** ◆

clue: pour

answer: come down in buckets

power *(n.)* **1.** force, STRENGTH, MIGHT, ENERGY, vigor, potency *the king's power* **2.** ABILITY, capacity, INFLUENCE *the power to succeed*

powerful *(adj.)* **1.** STRONG, forceful, mighty, potent, commanding *a powerful leader* **powerless,** WEAK **2.** muscular, hale, robust *a powerful runner*
(1) packing a punch

practice *(n.)* drill, training, exercise, EXPERIENCE, rehearsal

practice *(v.)* REHEARSE, PREPARE, REPEAT, recite, reiterate, drill

praise *(n.)* approval, HONOR, applause, tribute, commendation, acclaim

praise *(v.)* APPROVE, HONOR, COMPLIMENT, commend, FLATTER, credit, APPLAUD, CHEER, congratulate CONDEMN, **denounce,** DISAPPROVE, **reprimand**
pat on the back
PRAYS, PREYS

pray *(v.)* ADORE, WORSHIP, supplicate
PREY

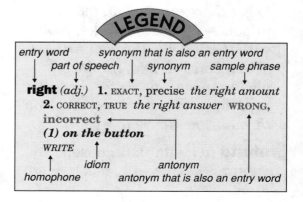

LEGEND

entry word   synonym that is also an entry word
    part of speech | synonym   sample phrase
↓   ↓   ↓   ↓
right *(adj.)* **1.** EXACT, precise *the right amount* **2.** CORRECT, TRUE *the right answer* WRONG, **incorrect** ←
(1) on the button
WRITE
↑   ↑   antonym
homophone   idiom   antonym that is also an entry word

93

precious (*adj.*) **1.** costly, priceless, VALUABLE *a precious jewel* **worthless, USELESS, trashy** **2.** beloved, DEAR, DARLING, cherished, prized *a precious child*

predict (*v.*) foresee, foretell, forecast, divine, prophesize

prefer (*v.*) FAVOR, CHOOSE, select, elect

prepare (*v.*) **1.** READY, CONDITION, TRAIN, PRACTICE *prepare for the Olympics* **2.** PROVIDE, FIX, COOK, ARRANGE, ORDER *prepare a meal*

present (*n.*) GIFT, PRIZE, FAVOR, offering, legacy, bequest, gratuity

present (*v.*) **1.** OFFER, GIVE, bestow, SHOW, PRODUCE *present an award* **2.** PERFORM, DISPLAY, EXHIBIT, STAGE *present a play* **3.** INTRODUCE *present a visitor*

preserve (*v.*) PROTECT, KEEP, MAINTAIN, GUARD, SAVE, safeguard, shield, CONSERVE **WASTE, squander**

press (*v.*) **1.** PUSH, depress, compress, SQUEEZE, flatten *Press the button.* **2.** hasten, HURRY *press to get there on time* **3.** URGE, impel, PERSUADE, provoke, motivate *Let's press the committee to take a vote.* **4.** BEG, implore, plead, appeal *press for forgiveness* **5.** CONTINUE, MOVE *press on through the dense forest*

pretend (*v.*) simulate, pose, AFFECT, DECEIVE, ACT, mock, feign

pretty (*adj.*) BEAUTIFUL, LOVELY, ATTRACTIVE, appealing, bonny, FAIR, HANDSOME **UGLY, homely, unsightly, PLAIN**

prevent (*v.*) **1.** hinder, impede, thwart, obstruct, INTERRUPT *prevent forest fires* **ENCOURAGE, incite, INSPIRE** **2.** BLOCK, prohibit, FORBID, disallow *prevent deer hunting* **ALLOW, PERMIT, grant** **(1) nip in the bud**

◆ Guess the Idiom ◆

clue: prevent

answer: nip in the bud

prey (*n.*) VICTIM, sufferer, scapegoat, quarry **predator, hunter** PRAY

price (*n.*) COST, VALUE, CHARGE, expense, FEE

pride (*n.*) self-respect, self-esteem, conceit, vanity, haughtiness **humility, humbleness** PRIED

print (*n.*) PICTURE, etching, lithograph, photograph, snapshot

print *(v.)* engrave, MARK, stamp

private *(adj.)* **1.** solitary, secluded *a private location* **2.** personal, individual, SECRET, concealed, CONFIDENTIAL *a private letter* PUBLIC, OPEN

prize *(n.)* FAVOR, GIFT, REWARD, AWARD, trophy, memento, bonus PRIES

probably *(adv.)* LIKELY, possibly, predictably

problem *(n.)* **1.** difficulty, handicap, disability, plight, setback, drawback, obstacle, misfortune, mishap, EMERGENCY, predicament, dilemma, crisis, quandary *a health problem* **2.** RIDDLE, PUZZLE, MYSTERY, enigma, paradox *Solve the problem.* **solution, explanation 3.** FAULT, DEFECT, flaw *the problem with the radio* **4.** MATTER, issue *consider your financial problem* *(2) can of worms*

produce *(v.)* **1.** CREATE, MAKE, INVENT, MANUFACTURE, CONSTRUCT, fabricate, originate *produce a new product.* **2.** BEAR, beget *produce a healthy baby* **3.** PROVIDE, FURNISH, render, DELIVER *produce a fine performance* **4.** SHOW, EXHIBIT *The attorney produced evidence in court*

product *(n.)* goods, merchandise, commodity, stock

profit *(n.)* gain, RETURN, benefit, advantage **loss, expenditure**

project *(n.)* **1.** PLAN, scheme, proposal, design *present a project for review* **2.** TASK, ACTIVITY, undertaking, venture *a good project for a rainy day*

promise *(n.)* oath, WORD, assurance, guarantee, pledge, vow

promise *(v.)* PLEDGE, vow, guarantee, ASSURE, AGREE *give one's word*

• Guess the Idiom •

clue: promise

answer: give one's word

pronounce *(v.)* **1.** utter, SPEAK, articulate *Pronounce the word correctly.* **2.** DECLARE, affirm *pronounce them husband and wife*

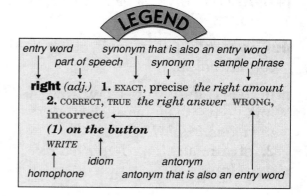

LEGEND

| entry word | synonym that is also an entry word |
| part of speech | synonym | sample phrase |

right *(adj.)* **1.** EXACT, precise *the right amount* **2.** CORRECT, TRUE *the right answer* WRONG, incorrect

(1) on the button

WRITE

homophone | idiom | antonym | antonym that is also an entry word

proof *(n.)* evidence, testimony, confirmation

proper *(adj.)* **1.** CORRECT, FIT, fitting, suitable, APPROPRIATE, applicable *the proper clothes* IMPROPER, **incorrect 2.** RIGHT, seemly, JUST, decent, respectable, virtuous *the proper thing to do* IMPROPER, **indecent**

property *(n.)* **1.** land, HOUSE, estate, acreage *buy a piece of property* **2.** belongings, holdings, assets *your personal property* **3.** feature, trait, CHARACTERISTIC, attribute *One property of water is that it is liquid.*

protect *(v.)* DEFEND, GUARD, SHELTER, harbor, PRESERVE, shield, screen ABANDON, DESERT, **forsake**
take under your wing

proud *(adj.)* NOBLE, stately, dignified, haughty, arrogant, boastful, supercilious HUMBLE, MODEST

prove *(v.)* CONVINCE, SATISFY, PERSUADE, SHOW, ESTABLISH, JUSTIFY, CONFIRM, verify, authenticate, attest **disprove**

provide *(v.)* GIVE, SUPPLY, furnish, PRODUCE **deprive**

public *(adj.)* SOCIAL, civil, civic, communal PRIVATE

pull *(v.)* **1.** haul, tug, DRAW, tow, lug, heave, JERK, wrench *Pull the wagon uphill.* PUSH **2.** strain, stretch *He pulled a muscle.*

pun *(n.)* JOKE, RIDDLE, jest, witticism

punch *(v.)* HIT, STRIKE, pound, BEAT, flog, smite, scourge

punish *(v.)* penalize, FINE, SCOLD, discipline, avenge, revenge, admonish, chastise, chasten, persecute, reprove REWARD, PRAISE
throw the book at, send up the river

◆ **Guess the Idiom** ◆

clue: punish

answer: throw the book at

pure *(adj.)* **1.** CLEAN, CLEAR, unpolluted, spotless, stainless, virgin, untouched, FRESH *pure water* **impure, polluted, contaminated 2.** INNOCENT, guiltless, virtuous, modest, decent, chaste *live a pure life* IMMORAL, WRONG, CORRUPT **3.** uniform, unmixed *pure silver* **4.** SHEER, absolute, unmitigated *pure happiness*

purpose *(n.)* GOAL, AIM, intent, OBJECT, objective, END, intention, REASON

push (*v.*) **1.** shove, thrust, press, FORCE, DRIVE, propel *Push him down.* PULL, DRAG **2.** jab, press *Push the button.* **3.** CONVINCE, ENCOURAGE, prod, INFLUENCE, URGE, incite, compel, impel, pressure *Push him to make a decision.*
(3) drive someone up the wall

put (*v.*) **1.** LAY, PLACE, SET, deposit, ARRANGE, LOCATE, LEAVE *Put the books on the table.* REMOVE, **withdraw 2.** thrust, THROW, launch *Put the rocket into space.* **3.** SAY, STATE, EXPRESS *put it mildly* **4.** apply *She put her design sense to good use.*

puzzle (*n.*) RIDDLE, MYSTERY, enigma, paradox
a hard nut to crack

puzzle (*v.*) CONFUSE, BAFFLE, bewilder, mix up, mislead, DISTURB, mystify, confound

Qq

• • • • • • • • • • • • • • • • • • • •

quaint (*adj.*) UNUSUAL, ODD, UNIQUE, STRANGE, peculiar COMMON, ORDINARY, **conventional**

quake (*v.*) SHAKE, VIBRATE, tremble, shudder, shiver, quiver

qualified (*adj.*) FIT, suited, ABLE, skilled, experienced, capable, competent, licensed, certified **unqualified, ill-suited, incompetent**

qualify (*v.*) fit, SUIT, LICENSE, certify

quality (*n.*) **1.** NATURE, trait, CHARACTERISTIC, PROPERTY *Her sweetness is an appealing quality.* **2.** excellence, CONDITION, stature, caliber *The quality of the photograph was excellent.*

quantity (*n.*) AMOUNT, SUM, TOTAL, extent

quarrel (*n.*) argument, disagreement, FIGHT, tiff, tussle, scrape, dispute, fracas
a war of words

quarrel (*v.*) squabble, bicker, clash, FIGHT, ARGUE, dispute, DISAGREE, tussle, wrangle, oppose, RESIST
have words, fight like cats and dogs

queer (*adj.*) ODD, STRANGE, WEIRD, UNUSUAL, peculiar, UNIQUE, uncommon, eccentric, quirkish, outlandish, questionable, abnormal, irregular, atypical **typical, ORDINARY, USUAL**

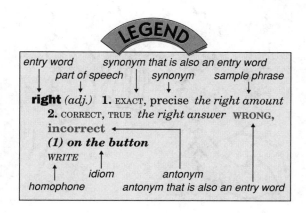

LEGEND

entry word   synonym that is also an entry word
    part of speech   synonym   sample phrase
right (*adj.*) **1.** EXACT, precise *the right amount* **2.** CORRECT, TRUE *the right answer* WRONG, **incorrect** ←
(1) on the button
WRITE
     idiom   antonym
homophone   antonym that is also an entry word

question (*n.*) REQUEST, appeal, plea, inquiry, entreaty ANSWER, **response, retort**

question (*v.*) **1.** interrogate, ASK, INQUIRE *question the suspect* ANSWER, RESPOND, **retort 2.** dispute, DOUBT, debate *question someone's judgment* **affirm (1) give the third degree**

quick (*adj.*) **1.** FAST, RAPID, speedy, swift, HASTY, fleet, nimble, brisk *a quick meal* SLOW, **gradual, sluggish 2.** SUDDEN, curt, abrupt, blunt *a quick decision* **delayed, postponed 3.** SMART, BRIGHT, INTELLIGENT, CLEVER, WITTY *a quick mind* DUMB, STUPID, **doltish**

quiet (*n.*) CALM, stillness, silence NOISE, **din, clamor**

quiet (*v.*) CALM, hush, silence, lull, muffle, stifle, suppress, subdue, quell **arouse, provoke**

quiet (*adj.*) **1.** SILENT, speechless, hushed, STILL, mute, dumb *a quiet audience* NOISY, LOUD, **clamorous 2.** CALM, STILL, inactive *quiet water* ACTIVE, **bustling 3.** CALM, passive, submissive, TAME, subdued, placid *a quiet horse* **spirited, lively, frisky 4.** SHY, reserved, bashful *a very quiet child* **outgoing, bold, confident**

Go **CRAZY** with **WORDS!**

quiet

quit (*v.*) **1.** STOP, discontinue *Quit talking.* CONTINUE, **proceed**
2. LEAVE, RESIGN, renounce, retire, relinquish, forsake, ABANDON, DESERT, abdicate *He quit his job.*
(1) call it a day (2) throw in the towel

quiz (*n.*) TEST, exam, examination, PUZZLE

quote (*v.*) **1.** cite, REPEAT, STATE *quote an author's work*
2. NAME, SET, ESTABLISH, MENTION *quote a price*

Rr

● ●

race (*n.*) **1.** breed, PEOPLE, tribe, nation *proud of one's color and race* **2.** CONTEST, MATCH, COMPETITION, meet, rivalry *Are you competing in the race?*

race (*v.*) **1.** RUSH, HURRY, HUSTLE, RUN, hasten, speed, DASH *She had to race to get things done.*
2. COMPETE *race against an opponent*

racket (*n.*) NOISE, hubbub, disturbance, din, uproar, clamor, commotion, tumult
RACQUET

rage (*n.*) **1.** ANGER, madness, frenzy, fury, wrath, fierceness, ferocity *The insult left her in a rage.*
2. fashion, fad, craze *Bell-bottom pants are the rage again.*

ragged (*adj.*) **1.** SHABBY, sloppy, unkempt, untidy, frumpish, scraggly *a ragged appearance*
2. jagged, serrated, barbed, irregular *She cut her finger on the ragged edge.*

raid (*n.*) invasion, ATTACK, assault, foray, onslaught, blitz

raid (*v.*) INVADE, ATTACK, assault, ambush, beset, STORM

rain (*n.*) drizzle, shower, sprinkle, spray, STORM, downpour, gale, flood, torrent, deluge
REIGN, REIN

raise (*v.*) **1.** LIFT, ELEVATE, SUPPORT, hoist *raise a flag* **lower, drop**
2. INCREASE, promote, heighten, awaken, arouse, spark, invigorate *raise interest in the community* DECREASE, **diminish**
3. REAR, breed *raise horses*
4. cultivate, GROW *raise tomatoes*
5. COLLECT, GATHER *raise money*
RAYS, RAZE

random (*adj.*) casual, disorganized, haphazard, serendipitous **organized, structured, systematic**

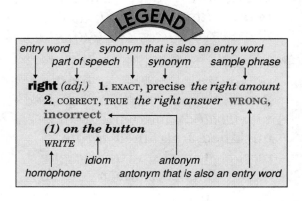

LEGEND

entry word — synonym that is also an entry word
part of speech — synonym — sample phrase
↓ ↓ ↓ ↓
right (*adj.*) **1.** EXACT, precise *the right amount*
2. CORRECT, TRUE *the right answer* WRONG, **incorrect** ←
(1) on the button
WRITE ↑
↑ idiom — antonym
homophone — antonym that is also an entry word

range *(n.)* SCOPE, extent, variance, SPACE, amplitude

rank *(n.)* standing, POSITION, STATION, status, CLASS, GRADE, level

rank *(v.)* ARRANGE, ORDER, classify, SORT

rank *(adj.)* ROTTEN, moldy, stinking, SOUR, FOUL, rancid, putrid

rapid *(adj.)* FAST, QUICK, swift, speedy, HASTY, fleeting, expeditious SLOW, **sluggish, gradual, deliberate**

rare *(adj.)* uncommon, SCARCE, UNUSUAL, distinctive COMMON, USUAL, ORDINARY, **plentiful**

rascal *(n.)* rogue, scoundrel, scamp, VILLAIN, knave

rate *(n.)* **1.** COST, CHARGE, PRICE, standard, valuation *pay the hourly rate* **2.** QUANTITY, AMOUNT, DEGREE *the rate of growth* **3.** SPEED, velocity, pace, tempo *The train travels at a rate of 100 miles per hour.*

rate *(v.)* **1.** PRICE, estimate, VALUE, appraise, evaluate, MEASURE, assess *Rate the cost of repairs.* **2.** evaluate, grade, CONSIDER, regard *Rate their skill.* **3.** DESERVE *rate special attention*

raw *(adj.)* **1.** uncooked, green, unripe *raw vegetables* **cooked** **2.** unfinished, CRUDE, unpolished *raw wood* **3.** inexperienced, unskilled, untrained *a raw recruit* **4.** irritated *a raw sore throat* **5.** COLD, DAMP *a raw day*

raze *(v.)* DESTROY, RUIN, demolish, obliterate **BUILD, CREATE** *RAYS, RAISE*

reach *(v.)* **1.** STRETCH, EXTEND *The rope reaches across the room.* **2.** accomplish, attain, EARN, FULFILL, realize *Strive to reach your goal.*

read *(v.)* STUDY, EXAMINE, peruse ***bury oneself in*** *REED*

◆ Guess the Idiom ◆

clue: read

answer: bury oneself in

ready *(adj.)* prepared, fitted, WILLING, disposed **unprepared, incomplete** ***in the saddle***

real *(adj.)* **1.** GENUINE, TRUE, CERTAIN, authentic, factual, valid *a real ruby* FAKE, **phony, counterfeit, bogus** **2.** actual, substantial, tangible, material *Are ghosts real?* IMAGINARY, **legendary**

realize *(v.)* COMPREHEND, UNDER-STAND, grasp, conceive, deter-mine, CONCLUDE, fathom
get through one's head, get the picture

rear *(n.)* BACK, tail, END, posterior FRONT, **face, anterior**

rear *(v.)* RAISE, foster, EDUCATE

reason *(n.)* **1.** CAUSE, motive, AIM, PURPOSE, stimulus *the reason for the meeting* **2.** explanation, EXCUSE, justification, rationale *the reason one is late*

reason *(v.)* THINK, JUDGE, CONSIDER, contemplate, deliber-ate, REFLECT

recall *(v.)* **1.** REMEMBER, recollect, reminisce, muse *I don't recall the exact number.* FORGET **2.** revoke, withdraw, CANCEL, retract, rescind, veto, override *The manufacturer recalled one of its models.* **enact, affirm**

receive *(v.)* GET, ACQUIRE, ACCEPT, inherit GIVE, PRESENT, **bestow**

recess *(n.)* BREAK, intermission, vacation, respite

recipe *(n.)* DIRECTIONS, formula, prescription

reckless *(adj.)* CARELESS, rash, negligent, foolhardy, HASTY, impetuous **CAREFUL, CAUTIOUS, prudent**

reckon *(v.)* THINK, CONSIDER, BELIEVE, regard, contemplate, suppose, surmise

recognize *(v.)* **1.** REMEMBER, KNOW, IDENTIFY, distinguish *I recognize the man in the picture.* **2.** ADMIT, acknowledge, APPRECIATE *I recog-nize I am wrong.*

recommend *(v.)* APPROVE, endorse, commend, sanction, advocate **disparage**

record *(n.)* LIST, register, chroni-cle, catalog, inventory, COPY

record *(v.)* WRITE, inscribe, register, ENTER

reduce *(v.)* LESSEN, DECREASE, SUB-TRACT, withdraw, deduct, CON-TRACT, DROP, dwindle, diminish, subside INCREASE, RAISE
make a dent in

reflect *(v.)* **1.** mirror, RETURN, REPRODUCE *reflect my image* **2.** THINK, CONSIDER, muse, medi-tate, deliberate *reflect on a dis-agreement* **3.** SHOW, DISPLAY, PRESENT, DEMONSTRATE, manifest *reflect a positive attitude*

refuse *(n.)* rubbish, GARBAGE, TRASH, WASTE, rubble, debris

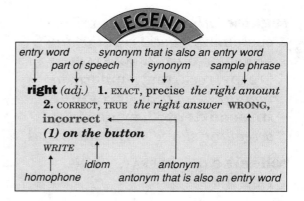

refuse *(v.)* decline, REJECT, DENY, repel, spurn **accept, admit** *turn down, put one's foot down*

regardless *(adv.)* notwithstanding, despite, besides

region *(n.)* AREA, district, quarter, territory, ZONE, sector

regret *(n.)* remorse, SORROW, CONCERN, grief, heartache, MISERY, DISTRESS, contrition, penitence

regret *(v.)* lament, repent, rue, bewail, deplore **rejoice** *cry over spilled milk*

• Guess the Idiom •

clue: regret

answer: cry over spilled milk

regular *(adj.)* **1.** USUAL, ordinary, customary *just a regular day* UNUSUAL, **odd 2.** CONSTANT, STEADY, recurrent, uniform *a regular heartbeat* **irregular, intermittent 3.** symmetrical *a regular shape* **asymmetrical**

rehearse *(v.)* REPEAT, recite, PRACTICE

reject *(v.)* **1.** decline, snub, REFUSE, DISCARD *reject the invitation* ACCEPT **2.** DISMISS, spurn, DENY, oust, expel, exile *reject the possibility of surprise* RECOGNIZE *(1) give the cold shoulder, leave out in the cold, turn thumbs down*

relax *(v.)* **1.** REST, PAUSE, lounge, loll, EASE, repose *relax with a book* **2.** loosen, slacken *relax your hold on the rope*

release *(v.)* FREE, loose, liberate, extricate CAPTURE, TRAP *let off the hook*

relief *(n.)* **1.** HELP, assistance, AID, SUPPORT *send relief to the victims* **2.** COMFORT, EASE *a feeling of relief*

religious *(adj.)* **1.** devout, HOLY, pious, reverent *a religious ceremony* **impious 2.** FAITHFUL, CONSISTENT, fervent, devoted *a religious fan* **fickle, changeable**

remain *(v.)* **1.** STAY, WAIT, REST *Remain at work.* LEAVE, **depart 2.** CONTINUE, LAST, abide, prevail *remain a loyal friend* **abandon, discontinue, forsake**

remark *(n.)* COMMENT, statement, utterance, SAYING, commentary

remark *(v.)* SAY, EXPRESS, utter

remember *(v.)* recollect, RECALL, RECOGNIZE, KNOW, MEMORIZE, retain FORGET *have on the tip of one's tongue*

remind *(v.)* prompt, SUGGEST
ring a bell

remove *(v.)* withdraw, TAKE, RID,
eliminate, extract **transfer,
retain, deposit**

repair *(v.)* FIX, PATCH, remedy,
restore, renew, mend, rectify
BREAK, **dismantle, impair**

repeat *(v.)* **1.** REPRODUCE, DUPLI-
CATE *Repeat the assignment.*
2. REHEARSE, PRACTICE, ECHO,
relate, report, reiterate *Repeat
the words to yourself.*
(2) hammer into one's head

• Guess the Idiom •

clue: repeat

answer: hammer into one's head

reply *(n.)* ANSWER, response,
acknowledgment, comeback,
reaction, rejoinder

reply *(v.)* ANSWER, RESPOND, retort
QUESTION, ASK

represent *(v.)* PICTURE, portray,
REPRODUCE, depict

reproduce *(v.)* REPEAT, DUPLICATE,
COPY

reputation *(n.)* CHARACTER, FAME,
renown, distinction, INFLUENCE,
prestige

request *(n.)* demand, appeal,
inquiry, entreaty

request *(v.)* ASK, solicit, appeal,
beseech DENY

require *(v.)* **1.** NEED, WANT *We
require food and water to live.*
2. DEMAND, DIRECT, INSIST, ORDER
*Require the children to make
their own beds.*

rescue *(v.)* **1.** FREE, SAVE, liberate
rescue the sailors ABANDON
2. recover, reclaim, restore,
IMPROVE *They work to rescue the
beaches from erosion.*

research *(v.)* STUDY, READ, EXAM-
INE, INVESTIGATE, EXPLORE

resign *(v.)* QUIT, forsake, LEAVE,
relinquish, renounce

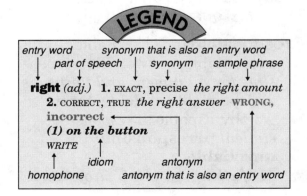

LEGEND

entry word   synonym that is also an entry word
   part of speech   synonym   sample phrase

right *(adj.)* **1.** EXACT, precise *the right amount*
2. CORRECT, TRUE *the right answer* WRONG,
incorrect
(1) on the button
WRITE
   idiom   antonym
homophone   antonym that is also an entry word

resist *(v.)* **1.** FIGHT, oppose, confront *Resist the enemy.* YIELD, SURRENDER **2.** IGNORE, STAND, withstand, thwart, curb *Resist the temptation.* **submit**
(1) make a stand, not give an inch

· Guess the Idiom ·

clue: resist

answer: make a stand

respect *(n.)* **1.** regard, HONOR, admiration, esteem, homage, deference *Respect your elders.* **2.** DETAIL, particular, feature, point *In one respect, your plan is solid.*

respect *(v.)* regard, esteem, HONOR, ADMIRE, venerate, revere

respond *(v.)* ANSWER, react, REPLY, retort QUESTION

responsible *(adj.)* **1.** liable, accountable, answerable *responsible for equipment and uniforms* **2.** dependable, reliable, trustworthy, capable *a responsible student* **irresponsible, unreliable**
(1) falling on one's shoulders

rest *(n.)* **1.** CALM, EASE, QUIET, relaxation, PAUSE *a rest in the storm* **2.** NAP, SLEEP, repose *Take a rest on the couch.* **3.** remainder, remnant, residue, surplus *Give the rest of the food to the dog.*

restaurant *(n.)* cafe, bistro, delicatessen, canteen, diner, luncheonette

restless *(adj.)* **1.** moving, unstable, wandering, roving *a restless child* QUIET, **sedate 2.** uneasy, NERVOUS, fretful, discontented, jittery, apprehensive, skittish *a restless mood* CALM, **relaxed 3.** sleepless, wakeful, insomnious *tired after a restless night's sleep*

result *(n.)* END, EFFECT, outcome, consequence, sequel CAUSE

result *(v.)* arise, FOLLOW, HAPPEN, ensue CAUSE

· Guess the Idiom ·

clue: responsible

answer: falling on one's shoulders

return (*v.*) **1.** reappear *The students return to the classroom.* **2.** restore, renew, revert *return to original condition* **3.** replace *Return the file to the drawer.* **4.** repay *Return the money.*

revenge (*n.*) retaliation, vengeance, reprisal, vendetta ***taste of one's own medicine, get even with***

reverse (*v.*) TURN, transpose, invert

review (*v.*) STUDY, reconsider, revise, EXAMINE, reexamine ***brush up on***

revolution (*n.*) **1.** revolt, rebellion, mutiny, uprising *the American Revolution* **2.** rotation, movement, circuit, cycle *one revolution around the sun*

reward (*n.*) PRIZE, bounty, FAVOR, AWARD, bonus, compensation **punishment, penalty**

rewrite (*v.*) revise, alter, edit, redraft, revamp

rich (*adj.*) **1.** wealthy, affluent, prosperous *my rich uncle* POOR, **penniless 2.** lavish, LUXURIOUS, extravagant, SPLENDID, sumptuous, opulent *a rich home* **modest, humble 3.** abundant, profuse *a rich harvest* **meager,** SPARE
(1) rolling in dough

rid (*v.*) **1.** FREE, CLEAR, RELEASE *Rid yourself of all your fears.* **2.** DESTROY, ELIMINATE *She got rid of the mosquitoes.*

• **Guess the Idiom** •

clue: rich

answer: rolling in dough

riddle (*n.*) PUZZLE, MYSTERY, PROBLEM, enigma, quandary ***can of worms***

ridicule (*v.*) INSULT, jeer, mock, TEASE, taunt, deride, satirize **praise, compliment**

ridiculous (*adj.*) FOOLISH, ABSURD, preposterous, laughable, ludicrous, inept **praiseworthy, sensible, commendable,** SOUND

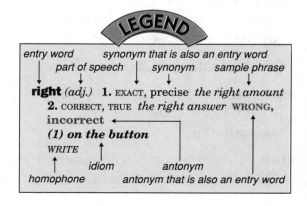

LEGEND

entry word   synonym that is also an entry word
   part of speech   synonym   sample phrase

right (*adj.*) **1.** EXACT, precise *the right amount* **2.** CORRECT, TRUE *the right answer* WRONG, **incorrect**
(1) on the button
WRITE
   idiom   antonym
homophone   antonym that is also an entry word

right *(n.)* **1.** privilege, due *the right to an attorney* **2.** CLAIM, ownership, title *the right to the property*
WRITE. RITE

right *(adj.)* **1.** EXACT, ACCURATE, precise *the right amount* **2.** CORRECT, TRUE *the right answer* WRONG, **incorrect,** FALSE **3.** FAIR, JUST, HONEST, upright, lawful, APPROPRIATE *the right thing to do*
(1) on the button
WRITE, RITE

rigid *(adj.)* STIFF, inflexible, unbending, STRICT, stern FLEXIBLE, **adaptable, elastic, pliable**

rim *(n.)* BORDER, EDGE, SIDE, brim, margin, skirt, fringe, verge

ring *(n.)* **1.** CIRCLE, hoop, loop *a plastic ring* **2.** GANG, BAND, clan, clique *a car theft ring*
WRING

ring *(v.)* **1.** chime, toll, peal, sound, tinkle *Ring the bell.* **2.** encircle, surround *The police ring the building.*
WRING

riot *(n.)* clash, STRUGGLE, disturbance, tumult, BRAWL, revolt, uproar, fray, fracas

rip *(v.)* slash, slit, SPLIT, rend

ripe *(adj.)* READY, mature, finished, aged RAW, **green, immature**

rise *(v.)* **1.** ELEVATE, arise, ascend *The dough will rise.* FALL, SINK, DESCEND **2.** INCREASE, ADD, CLIMB, mount, AMOUNT, ascend *The population will rise.* DECREASE **3.** arise, WAKE, get up *rise in the morning*

risk *(n.)* CHANCE, jeopardy, DANGER, HAZARD, peril
a long shot

risk *(v.)* BET, GAMBLE, CHANCE, stake, wager, venture, DARE
play with fire, stick your neck out, go out on a limb

rival *(n.)* competitor, OPPONENT, ENEMY, FOE, antagonist, adversary **teammate, partner**

road *(n.)* STREET, lane, avenue, boulevard, passage, alley, WAY, track, ROUTE, COURSE
RODE

roam *(v.)* WANDER, range, rove, ramble, meander, traipse

rob *(v.)* STEAL, loot, sack, rifle, STRIP, RAID, fleece, pilfer, despoil, deprive, divest, ravage

robber *(n.)* bandit, THIEF, outlaw, crook, CRIMINAL, burglar, pickpocket, brigand, pirate

rock *(n.)* **1.** STONE, pebble, boulder *The sailboat was wrecked on the rocks.* **2.** mineral, gem, ore *Diamonds and rubies may be called rocks.*

rock *(v.)* sway, swing, wobble, totter, reel, oscillate

rod *(n.)* pole, STICK, wand, cane, staff, scepter

role (n.) **1.** PART, CHARACTER, position *the starring role* **2.** DUTY, TASK, function *your office role*
ROLL

roll (n.) **1.** bun, bread, loaf *Butter the roll.* **2.** TURN, SPIN, somersault, flip *Do a forward roll.*
ROLE

roll (v.) **1.** TURN, whirl, revolve, rotate *Roll the wheel.* **2.** bind, WRAP, swathe *Roll the rug.*
ROLE

romantic (adj.) **1.** fictional, imaginative *a romantic tale*
2. amorous, passionate, sentimental, lovelorn, TENDER, SENSITIVE *in a romantic mood*

roof (n.) COVER, canopy, SHELTER

room (n.) **1.** AREA, SPACE, extent, expanse *room for one more*
2. ward, apartment, chamber *the storage room*

root (n.) **1.** tuber, rootlet *the root of a tree* **2.** CAUSE, origin, beginning, SOURCE, basis, REASON, derivation *the root of her anger*

rot (v.) SPOIL, DECAY, decompose, putrefy, molder

rotten (adj.) **1.** decayed, stinking, FOUL, rancid, RANK, SOUR, moldy, putrid *a rotten piece of meat* FRESH **2.** DISHONEST, CORRUPT, treacherous *He played a rotten trick.*

rough (adj.) **1.** uneven, bumpy, rocky, COARSE, bristly *a rough texture* SMOOTH **2.** RUDE, HARSH, uncivil, IMPOLITE, churlish *rough manners* POLITE **3.** stormy, tempestuous *rough weather* CALM **4.** HARD, DIFFICULT, TOUGH *a rough test* EASY
RUFF

round (adj.) curved, circular, spherical, globular

route (n.) WAY, COURSE, PATH, ROAD
ROOT

royal (adj.) NOBLE, MAJESTIC, regal, imperial, kingly

rub (v.) **1.** stroke, massage, knead, stimulate *rub someone's back*
2. WIPE, polish, scour, SCRUB, scrape *Rub off the tarnish.*

rude (adj.) blunt, gruff, curt, discourteous, IMPOLITE, churlish, impertinent, insolent, impudent, flippant, boorish POLITE, **courteous, gracious**

rugged (adj.) hardy, STURDY, robust, TOUGH, durable, stalwart FRAGILE, **delicate,** WEAK

ruin (v.) mar, SPOIL, tarnish, deface, disfigure, DESTROY, demolish, defile, debase, impair

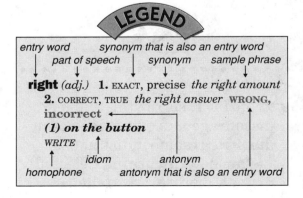

LEGEND

entry word — synonym that is also an entry word
part of speech — synonym — sample phrase
right (adj.) **1.** EXACT, precise *the right amount*
2. CORRECT, TRUE *the right answer* WRONG, incorrect
(1) on the button
WRITE
homophone — idiom — antonym — antonym that is also an entry word

rule *(n.)* LAW, ORDER, regulation, statute, mandate, principle, standard, doctrine, decree, tenet, precept

rule *(v.)* GOVERN, reign, CONTROL, COMMAND, MANAGE, dominate **call the tune, hold sway**

ruler *(n.)* LEADER, CHIEF, head, monarch, KING, emperor, czar, lord, sovereign, president

rumor *(n.)* GOSSIP, hearsay FACT

run *(v.)* **1.** jog, HURRY, scurry, RUSH, DASH, dart, sprint, RACE, bound, bolt, trot, canter, gallop, lope *run down a street* **2.** ESCAPE, flee, abscond *run from the law* REMAIN, STAY **3.** OPERATE, WORK, MANAGE *run a machine*

rural *(adj.)* COUNTRY, rustic, pastoral, agrarian, agricultural **urban, citified**

rush *(v.)* HURRY, hasten, speed, DASH, HUSTLE, scurry, scoot, sprint **dally, delay** **beat the pavement, shake a leg**

rusty *(adj.)* corroded, WORN

Ss

sad *(adj.)* **1.** sorrowful, UNHAPPY, discouraged, GLOOMY, downcast, dispirited, somber, GLUM, BLUE, melancholy, mournful, dejected, dismal, morose, crestfallen, despondent, doleful, woeful, forlorn, woebegone *sad feelings* HAPPY, **joyful, fortunate, contented,** GLAD, **ecstatic,** CHEERFUL **2.** POOR, MISERABLE, wretched *a sad state of affairs* GOOD, VALUABLE **(1) down in the dumps**

safe *(adj.)* **1.** protected, guarded, SECURE, exempt, invulnerable *a safe place to hide* **endangered, unsafe,** DANGEROUS, **exposed, hazardous 2.** SURE, reliable, trustworthy *a safe plan of action* RISKY, **uncertain (1) out of the woods**

◆ **Guess the Idiom** ◆

clue: rush

answer: beat the pavement

safety *(n.)* security, protection, preservation, invulnerability DANGER, **peril**

sail *(v.)* **1.** float, cruise, skim, coast, navigate, embark *sail across a lake* **2.** pilot, STEER, navigate *sail a boat* SALE

same *(adj.)* ALIKE, similar, matched, EQUAL, equivalent, IDENTICAL, uniform, indistinguishable DIFFERENT, **dissimilar, unalike**

sample *(n.)* example, PATTERN, model, specimen, COPY, prototype

sample *(v.)* TASTE, TRY, EXPERIENCE, TEST

sane *(adj.)* SOUND, lucid, rational, sensible CRAZY, **insane**

satisfactory *(adj.)* **1.** acceptable, pleasing *a satisfactory meal* **2.** sufficient, ADEQUATE, ample, enough *a satisfactory amount*

satisfy *(v.)* **1.** PLEASE, gratify *satisfy a desire* **2.** FILL, sate, satiate *satisfy an appetite*

savage *(adj.)* **1.** BRUTAL, VIOLENT, FEROCIOUS, fierce, cold-blooded *a savage attack* **2.** WILD, uncivilized, barbarous *a savage person*

save *(v.)* **1.** RESCUE, liberate, DELIVER *save the victim* **2.** KEEP, STORE, PRESERVE, secure, accumulate, HOLD, hoard, reserve, amass *save money* SPEND, **squander** *(2) squirrel away*

say *(v.)* TELL, STATE, CLAIM, DECLARE, MENTION, refer, REMARK, recite, ANNOUNCE, notify, disclose, divulge, assert, proclaim, profess, vouch, attest *put into words*

saying *(n.)* motto, phrase, slogan, expression, proverb, catchword, maxim, axiom, adage

scanty *(adj.)* meager, sparing, sparse **abundant, profuse**

scarce *(adj.)* RARE, uncommon, infrequent, wanting, SCANTY, deficient COMMON, **abundant, PLENTIFUL**

scare *(v.)* FRIGHTEN, startle, ALARM, SHOCK, daunt, THREATEN, BULLY, terrify, dismay, menace, intimidate ASSURE, CALM, SOOTHE
make one's hair stand on end

◆ Guess the Idiom ◆

clue: scare

answer: make one's hair stand on end

scary *(adj.)* frightening, spooky, terrifying, horrifying

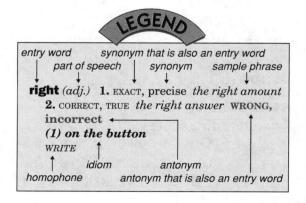

LEGEND

entry word   synonym that is also an entry word
    part of speech   synonym   sample phrase

right *(adj.)* **1.** EXACT, precise *the right amount* **2.** CORRECT, TRUE *the right answer* WRONG, incorrect ←
(1) on the button
WRITE

homophone   idiom   antonym
    antonym that is also an entry word

scatter *(v.)* **1.** strew, sprinkle, disperse, SPREAD, DISTRIBUTE *Scatter the seeds.* GATHER **2.** disperse, disband, SEPARATE, DISSOLVE *The crowd began to scatter.*

scene *(n.)* VIEW, landscape, survey, vision

scent *(n.)* SMELL, odor, fragrance, aroma, PERFUME, essence, bouquet **stench**

school *(n.)* institute, academy, COLLEGE, university

scold *(v.)* reprimand, BLAME, chide, reproach, rebuke, reprove, berate
give someone a piece of your mind

***clue:* scold**

answer: give someone a piece of your mind

scope *(n.)* RANGE, extent

scramble *(v.)* **1.** HURRY, RUSH, skedaddle, scurry *He scrambled to get ready for work.* **2.** MIX, BLEND, COMBINE, merge *Scramble the eggs.* **3.** COMPETE, STRUGGLE, vie *The children scramble for first place in line.*

scrap *(n.)* BIT, fragment, morsel, remnant, particle, crumb

scrap *(v.)* DISCARD, ABANDON, forsake, demolish **retain**

scream *(v.)* CRY, screech, shriek, SHOUT
yell one's head off, blow your stack

***clue:* scream**

answer: yell one's head off

scribble *(v.)* scrawl, jot, doodle, WRITE

scrub *(v.)* scour, clean, swab

seal *(v.)* CLOSE, FASTEN, secure OPEN, RELEASE, **unlock**

search *(n.)* HUNT, quest, pursuit, CHASE, exploration

search *(v.)* SEEK, EXAMINE, scan, INVESTIGATE, INSPECT, scrutinize, probe, HUNT, EXPLORE, INVESTIGATE, rummage, rifle
go through with a fine-tooth comb, leave no stone unturned

secret *(n.)* MYSTERY, CONFIDENCE

secret *(adj.)* **1.** PRIVATE, personal, individual, SPECIAL *a secret diary* PUBLIC, **disclosed, known** **2.** stealthy, mysterious, unknown, HIDDEN, concealed, clandestine, furtive, surreptitious, obscure *a secret plan* **shared, accessible,** OPEN *(2) keeping something under one's hat*

section *(n.)* PART, PIECE, portion, segment, division, FRACTION, component, feature, department

secure *(adj.)* **1.** SAFE, protected, guarded, invulnerable *a secure hiding place* **unsafe,** OPEN, precarious **2.** CONFIDENT, self-confident, poised, sanguine *a secure person* INSECURE, **doubtful**

◆ **Guess the Idiom** ◆

clue: secret

answer: keeping something under one's hat

Go **CRAZY** with **WORDS!**

scent

see *(v.)* **1.** NOTE, NOTICE, OBSERVE, perceive, distinguish, DISCOVER, discern, DETECT, SPOT, behold, regard, picture, IMAGINE *see the bird take off* IGNORE, **disregard** **2.** UNDERSTAND, APPRECIATE, EXPERIENCE *see the truth* **3.** accompany, escort *see her to the door* **(1) lay eyes on**
SEA

seek *(v.)* **1.** SEARCH, LOOK, INVESTIGATE *seek someone in hiding* **2.** ATTEMPT, TRY, strive, endeavor *seek to improve their living conditions*

seem *(v.)* APPEAR, LOOK
SEAM

selfish *(adj.)* CHEAP, miserly, STINGY, inconsiderate, heedless, THOUGHTLESS, CARELESS **selfless, GENEROUS**

sell *(v.)* vend, market, peddle, hawk, retail, exchange, barter BUY, **acquire, purchase**
CELL

send *(v.)* post, mail, ship, dispatch, transmit, forward, CONVEY
RECEIVE

sense *(n.)* **1.** FEELING, sensation, perception, impression *a sense of fear* **2.** REASON, JUDGMENT, conviction, MIND, understanding, intellect *use common sense*
CENTS

sensitive *(adj.)* **1.** touchy, testy, temperamental, MOODY, peevish *a sensitive talk* **2.** vulnerable, susceptible *sensitive to criticism*

hardened, indifferent **3.** TENDER, painful *a sensitive bruise*

separate *(v.)* PART, DIVIDE, sever, DETACH, DISCONNECT **ATTACH, JOIN, CONNECT**

separate *(adj.)* apart, isolated, SINGLE, lone, remote **ATTACHED, connected, joined,** UNITED

serious *(adj.)* **1.** solemn, EARNEST, SOBER, GRIM, staid, ardent *a serious movie* **light, playful, funny 2.** GRAVE, CRITICAL, weighty, severe *a serious medical problem* **unimportant**

serve *(v.)* AID, HELP, ASSIST, oblige, SATISFY, PLEASE

set *(n.)* **1.** setting, scene, backdrop *the set for a play* **2.** COLLECTION, GROUP, BUNCH *a set of dishes*

set *(v.)* **1.** PUT, PLACE, LOCATE, LAY *Set it down on the table.* **2.** FIX, ESTABLISH, SETTLE, determine, regulate, ADJUST *Set the price.*

set *(adj.)* FIRM, unchanging, unyielding, adamant *carved in stone*

settle *(v.)* **1.** LIVE, abide, INHABIT *settle in a new town* **2.** PAY, compensate, remit, square *settle a debt*

several *(adj.)* SOME, various, MANY **few**

sew *(v.)* stitch, mend, darn, PATCH, embroider, suture
SO

shabby *(adj.)* SORRY, WORN, run-down, wretched, threadbare, RAGGED

shake *(v.)* **1.** QUAKE, tremble, shudder, rattle, shiver, twitch, quiver, VIBRATE, jolt, jar, rouse, oscillate *shake with fear* **2.** agitate *Shake the bottle of juice before you drink it.*

shame *(n.)* disgrace, dishonor, ignominy, embarrassment, humiliation, guilt, remorse PRIDE, HONOR

shape *(n.)* FORM, outline, PATTERN, FIGURE, mold, silhouette

share *(n.)* PART, PIECE, portion, serving, division, dividend WHOLE

share *(v.)* DIVIDE, DISTRIBUTE, apportion, allot

sharp *(adj.)* **1.** cutting, piercing *a sharp knife* **blunt**, DULL **2.** keen, SENSITIVE, QUICK, ALERT *A dog has sharp senses.* DULL, SLOW, **dense 3.** CLEVER, astute, shrewd *a sharp detective* STUPID, **dim-witted 4.** SEVERE, SERIOUS, acute, INTENSE, agonizing, excruciating *a sharp pain*

sheer *(adj.)* **1.** PURE, utter, CLEAR, absolute *sheer delight* **2.** THIN, FINE, CLEAR, transparent, diaphanous *sheer cloth* **opaque** *SHEAR*

shelter *(n.)* SAFETY, haven, retreat, ROOF, asylum, refuge, sanctuary EXPOSE, **reveal**

shelter *(v.)* HIDE, PROTECT, DEFEND, shield, screen

shine *(n.)* gloss, sheen, glaze, polish, luster

shine *(v.)* **1.** glisten, SPARKLE, shimmer, GLOW, glimmer, dazzle *The moonlight shines on the lake.* **2.** polish, burnish *Shine the car.*

shock *(n.)* **1.** surprise, astonishment, awe, bewilderment *the shock of seeing something disappear* **2.** CRASH, impact, collision *The shock cracked the axle.* **3.** jolt, paralysis *an electric shock*

shock *(v.)* **1.** AMAZE, SURPRISE, ASTONISH, stagger *The magic trick will shock you.* **2.** OFFEND, UPSET, disgust, outrage, appall *The violence in the film may shock you.* **3.** electrify, stun *Don't touch a live wire; it will shock you.*
(1) raise some eyebrows

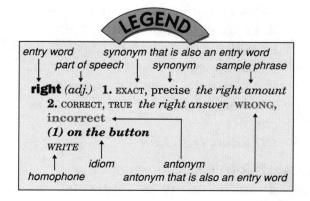

113

shocked *(adj.)* **1.** amazed, startled, astonished, staggered, appalled, aghast *shocked by her honesty* **2.** alarmed, unnerved, frightened *shocked by the news*
*(1) **can't believe one's eyes***

short *(adj.)* **1.** BRIEF, concise, condensed, succinct *a short story* LONG, **lengthy 2.** LITTLE, SMALL, puny *a short man* TALL, **towering 3.** RUDE, terse, brusque, pithy *He spoke in a short manner.* POLITE, FRIENDLY

shorten *(v.)* condense, CONCENTRATE, DECREASE, crop, SHRINK, abridge, abbreviate, REDUCE, diminish **lengthen**, ENLARGE, SWELL, GROW, INCREASE

shout *(v.)* YELL, CALL, DECLARE, EXCLAIM, SCREAM, shriek **whisper, murmur**
raise the roof

show *(n.)* **1.** exhibit, exhibition, DISPLAY, PLAY, performance, production, program *The show begins at 8:00.* **2.** sight, spectacle *The fireworks show was dazzling.*

show *(v.)* **1.** DEMONSTRATE, TEACH *show someone how to draw* **2.** LEAD, reveal, indicate, POINT, PRESENT, GUIDE, usher, EXPOSE, UNCOVER *show the way* CONCEAL, HIDE, **mask 3.** PROVE, manifest, disclose *show that the answer is correct*
*(2) **shed light on***

shrink *(v.)* LESSEN, REDUCE, dwindle, minimize, SHORTEN,

diminish, condense, CONTRACT, CONCENTRATE, abridge, abbreviate EXPAND, INCREASE, ENLARGE

shut *(v.)* CLOSE, secure, SEAL, slam, FASTEN, LOCK OPEN, **unfasten**

shy *(adj.)* bashful, TIMID, modest, coy, reserved, shrinking, retiring, demure, diffident, sheepish BOLD, **outgoing, forthright, outspoken, overt, brazen**

sick *(adj.)* ILL, ailing, unwell, diseased, unhealthy, infirm, FEEBLE, indisposed WELL, HEALTHY
under the weather

◆ **Guess the Idiom** ◆

clue: sick

answer: under the weather

sickness *(n.)* illness, DISEASE, ailment, malady, affliction

side *(n.)* **1.** EDGE, BORDER, margin, verge *the side of the paper* **2.** TEAM, faction *Which side are you rooting for?*
SIGHED

side *(v.)* SUPPORT, JOIN, advocate, CHAMPION, sanction
SIGHED

sign *(n.)* **1.** NOTICE, advertisement, poster, BILL, handbill, placard *Hang up the sign.* **2.** indication, HINT, symptom *a sign of the flu* **3.** MARK, token, SYMBOL *a sign that someone had been there*

sign *(v.)* endorse, initial, inscribe, autograph

silent *(adj.)* **1.** QUIET, soundless, STILL, CALM, sedate, placid, pacific *The house was silent.* LOUD, NOISY **2.** unexpressed, unstated, inferred, understood, implicit, insinuated *a silent agreement* **3.** inactive, passive, dormant, resting, lifeless, inanimate *The volcano was silent.*

silly *(adj.)* FOOLISH, senseless, RIDICULOUS, ABSURD, daft, idiotic, fatuous, frivolous, trifling, imprudent, inept, preposterous, asinine **reasonable, sensible**

simple *(adj.)* **1.** PLAIN, unadorned, ORDINARY, unaffected *a simple design* ELABORATE **2.** EASY, effortless, CLEAR *a simple recipe* DIFFICULT, COMPLEX **3.** naive, unsophisticated, inexperienced, FOOLISH *a simple child* **(2) a real snap**

sincere *(adj.)* HONEST, frank, OPEN, candid, direct, TRUE, REAL, GENUINE INSINCERE, **dishonest**

sing *(v.)* chant, carol, hum, vocalize, warble, croon

single *(adj.)* **1.** lone, sole, solitary, ALONE *a single cabin in the* *woods* **multiple** **2.** unmarried, unwed *a single man*

sink *(v.)* **1.** submerge, submerse, immerse *sink to the bottom of the river* **float, emerge,** RISE **2.** LESSEN, REDUCE, depress, plummet, plunge *The prices will sink.* INCREASE, **grow**

sit *(v.)* **1.** REST, PAUSE, REMAIN, repose *Sit for a while.* **2.** perch, settle, roost, squat *Sit on the chair.*

size *(n.)* bulk, volume, mass, extent, AMOUNT, gauge, SCOPE, magnitude, dimension *SIGHS*

sketch *(v.)* DRAW, portray, picture, ILLUSTRATE, outline, draft, REPRESENT, trace, depict

skill *(n.)* ABILITY, talent, knack, aptitude, expertise, adroitness

skin *(n.)* **1.** hide, fur, pelt, coat *the skin of a bear* **2.** rind, husk, PEEL, crust *the skin of an orange*

skinny *(adj.)* THIN, LEAN, slender, slight, underweight, lank, spare, gaunt FAT, **obese**, CHUBBY

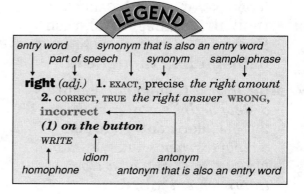

entry word   *synonym that is also an entry word*
   part of speech   *synonym*   *sample phrase*

right *(adj.)* **1.** EXACT, precise *the right amount* **2.** CORRECT, TRUE *the right answer* WRONG, **incorrect**
(1) on the button
WRITE

homophone   *idiom*   *antonym*   *antonym that is also an entry word*

skip *(v.)* **1.** HOP, JUMP, SPRING, LEAP, gambol *skip down the sidewalk* **2.** MISS, OMIT, disregard *skip a word* INCLUDE

slant *(n.)* diagonal, SLOPE, pitch, angle, ramp, gradient

slave *(n.)* vassal, pawn, captive, serf **master**

sleep *(v.)* slumber, NAP, DOZE, snooze, repose WAKE
hit the sack, hit the hay

slim *(adj.)* **1.** THIN, SKINNY, slender, gaunt, lank, svelte, lithe *a slim man* FAT, **corpulent, plump,** CHUBBY **2.** SMALL, trifling, insignificant *a slim chance for survival*

slip *(n.)* ERROR, MISTAKE, BLUNDER, oversight, offense, failing

slip *(v.)* slide, glide, skid, stumble

slope *(n.)* SLANT, pitch, angle, incline, tilt, ramp, gradient

slope *(v.)* TIP, LEAN, incline, slant, tilt

sloppy *(adj.)* **1.** MESSY, untidy, disordered, DIRTY, slovenly, unkempt, disheveled *a sloppy room* NEAT, TIDY **2.** CARELESS, THOUGHTLESS, neglectful, rash *Her work was sloppy.* CAREFUL, **painstaking, thoughtful**

slow *(adj.)* **1.** sluggish, leisurely *a slow walk* FAST, **speedy, swift** **2.** DULL, deficient, retarded *a slow learner* QUICK, SHARP, BRIGHT **3.** GRADUAL *a slow improvement* **abrupt**

sly *(adj.)* CUNNING, shrewd, crafty, artful, astute, wily, furtive

small *(adj.)* **1.** LITTLE, TINY, wee, puny, minute, compact, miniature, diminutive *a small animal* BIG, HUGE, **colossal, gigantic** **2.** slight, SCANT *a small amount of money* **3.** modest, MINOR, trivial, UNIMPORTANT *a small effort* IMPORTANT

smart *(adj.)* **1.** INTELLIGENT, BRIGHT, WISE, shrewd, CUNNING, ALERT, SHARP, apt, quick-witted, CLEVER, astute, canny, BRILLIANT, ingenious *a smart child* DUMB, STUPID, DULL, **dimwitted** **2.** stylish, neat, fashionable, trendy, modish, swanky, dapper *a smart dress* **dowdy, old-fashioned**

smash *(v.)* CRUSH, compress, shatter, demolish REPAIR

smell *(n.)* odor, aroma, SCENT, whiff, fragrance, extract, stench, essence, bouquet

smell *(v.)* **1.** sniff, inhale, BREATHE, whiff *Smell the rose.* **2.** STINK, reek, putrefy *Rotten eggs smell.*

smile *(v.)* grin, smirk, beam FROWN, **scowl**

smooth *(adj.)* **1.** EVEN, FLAT, LEVEL *Skate on the smooth sidewalk.* **uneven, bumpy, wrinkled,** ROUGH **2.** polished, slippery, slick, sleek *slip on the smooth surface* ROUGH **3.** creamy *Mix the batter until it is smooth.*

sneak *(v.)* slink, creep, prowl, STEAL, skulk, lurk

Go **CRAZY** with **WORDS!**

smell

sneaky *(adj.)* shifty, foxy, deceitful, furtive, covert, devious

soak *(v.)* drench, steep, immerse, submerge DRY

sober *(adj.)* **1.** temperate, abstemious *The alcoholic will work hard to stay sober.* intoxicated, DRUNK **2.** SERIOUS, somber *a sober occasion* frivolous

social *(adj.)* **1.** FRIENDLY, gregarious, convivial *a very social person* **2.** PUBLIC *a social setting*

soft *(adj.)* **1.** fleecy, fluffy, limp, FLEXIBLE, pliable, malleable *soft to the touch* HARD, STIFF, RIGID **2.** lenient *a soft attitude toward youthful offenders* STUBBORN, unyielding, HARSH **3.** MILD, GENTLE *a soft detergent*

solve *(v.)* EXPLAIN, decode, unravel, resolve, decipher *get to the bottom of*

some *(adj.)* SEVERAL, various
MANY
SUM

song *(n.)* TUNE, jingle, melody, music, refrain, anthem

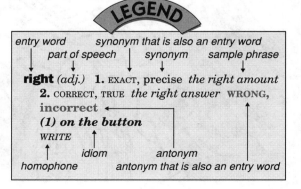

LEGEND

entry word   *synonym that is also an entry word*
   part of speech   *synonym*   *sample phrase*

right *(adj.)* **1.** EXACT, precise *the right amount* **2.** CORRECT, TRUE *the right answer* WRONG, incorrect ←
(1) on the button
WRITE

homophone   *idiom*   *antonym*
     antonym that is also an entry word

117

soothe (v.) **1.** EASE, CURE, COMFORT, appease *The medicine soothes the pain.* AGGRAVATE, **worsen, intensify 2.** CALM, QUIET, pacify, cajole *soothe someone's temper* **rouse, provoke, harass**
(2) take the edge off

sophisticated (adj.) experienced, suave, civilized, urbane CRUDE, **unrefined,** INNOCENT, **naive**

sore (n.) WOUND, CUT, affliction, infection, boil
SOAR

sore (adj.) painful, TENDER, irritated, hurt, infected
SOAR

sorrow (n.) grief, PAIN, REGRET, woe, sadness, heartache, MISERY, DISTRESS, remorse, anguish HAPPINESS, **gaiety, joy**

sorry (adj.) **1.** remorseful, apologetic, HUMBLE, repentant, penitent, contrite *I feel sorry for the trouble I have caused.* **2.** MISERABLE, SHABBY, wretched *The house was in sorry condition.* EXCELLENT, **superior,** SPLENDID

sort (n.) TYPE, KIND, CLASS, VARIETY, species

sort (v.) ORDER, classify, ARRANGE, DISTRIBUTE

sound (n.) NOISE, tone, din, racket

Go **CRAZY** with **WORDS!**

sound

sound (adj.) **1.** TRUE, CORRECT, reasonable, rational, sensible *a sound argument* faulty **2.** well, HEALTHY, hale *He felt sound enough to compete.* **unsound, unhealthy**

sour (v.) SPOIL, ferment, curdle

sour (adj.) **1.** tart, SHARP, BITTER, acidic, pungent *a sour apple* sweet **2.** brooding, crabby, dour, sullen, grumpy *a sour mood*

source (n.) ROOT, CAUSE, beginning, origin, derivation

souvenir (n.) keepsake, memento, token, relic, vestige

space (n.) **1.** ROOM, leeway, AREA, extent, capacity *enough space to fit one more* **2.** heavens, cosmos, universe, firmament *travel into outer space* **3.** opening, gap, cleft, interval, void *Leave a space between the desks.*

spare (v.) FORGIVE, PARDON, RELEASE, CLEAR, absolve PUNISH

spare (adj.) EXTRA, reserve, surplus, supplemental

sparkle (v.) glitter, glisten, twinkle, scintillate

speak (v.) **1.** SAY, PRONOUNCE, articulate *Speak your lines.* **2.** TELL, utter, EXPRESS, DECLARE, spout, rant *Speak the truth.* **3.** chat, chatter, converse, GOSSIP, prattle *Speak with a friend.*

spear (n.) lance, javelin

special (adj.) **1.** distinct, UNUSUAL, RARE, unique *Seeing a fox in the forest is a special experience.* commonplace **2.** significant, memorable, earthshaking, pressing *a special awards ceremony* **3.** EXTRAORDINARY, spectacular, astounding, overwhelming, impressive, breathtaking, WONDERFUL, FANTASTIC *The astronauts' landing on the moon was a special event.* ORDINARY, USUAL

speech (n.) **1.** LECTURE, address, TALK, utterance, discourse, oration *give a speech* **2.** LANGUAGE, dialect, articulation, talk *Dogs and cats lack speech.*

speed (n.) haste, swiftness, velocity

spell (n.) **1.** MAGIC, POWER, charm, incantation *under the wizard's spell* **2.** period, interval, TIME *a rainy spell*

spell (v.) WRITE, decipher, encode

spend (v.) **1.** expend, disperse, donate, CONTRIBUTE, squander, fritter, EXHAUST *spend money* SAVE, CONSERVE **2.** PASS, USE, consume *spend time on a farm*

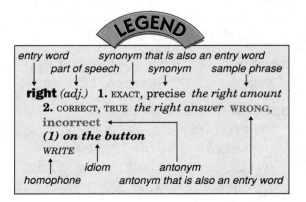

119

spicy *(adj.)* HOT, pungent, STRONG, SHARP, piquant MILD, BLAND

spin *(v.)* TURN, rotate, revolve, whirl, twist, swirl, reel, gyrate

spirit *(n.)* **1.** COURAGE, ENERGY, vitality *the fighting spirit* **2.** GHOST, vision, spook, specter, phantom, apparition *Can you see the spirit?*

spite *(n.)* venom, malice, resentment, rancor, pique, enmity, animosity **affection, goodwill**

splendid *(adj.)* stately, MAJESTIC, GRAND, MAGNIFICENT, GORGEOUS, sumptuous **dreadful**

split *(n.)* CRACK, fissure, breach

split *(v.)* **1.** cleave, halve, bisect, slice, sever, rend *split a log* CONNECT, JOIN **2.** SHARE, DIVIDE, DISTRIBUTE *split a pizza*

spoil *(v.)* **1.** BOTCH, fumble, BUNGLE, muff, RUIN, mar, HARM, DESTROY, defile *spoil a game* **2.** DECAY, decompose, putrefy, molder *The milk will spoil.*

spoon *(n.)* scoop, ladle, dipper

spot *(n.)* STAIN, blot, blotch, flaw, speck, blemish, pimple, DEFECT, imperfection

spot *(v.)* SEE, NOTICE, NOTE, OBSERVE, DETECT, discern, RECOGNIZE

spread *(v.)* **1.** INCREASE, MULTIPLY, STRETCH, EXPAND, REPRODUCE, propagate *The bird spreads its wings.* REDUCE, DECREASE **2.** DISTRIBUTE, PASS, TELL, ANNOUNCE, divulge, circulate *Spread the news.* **withhold,** CONCEAL **3.** SCATTER, disperse, strew, sprinkle *Spread the seeds.* GATHER, **collect 4.** smear, daub *Spread the jelly on the bread.*

spring *(v.)* **1.** LEAP, bound, JUMP *spring over a rock* **2.** emerge, originate *spring from within*

spy *(n.)* agent, scout, informer, snoop, investigator

spy *(v.)* SEE, behold, DETECT, DISCOVER, OBSERVE, INVESTIGATE

squeeze *(v.)* **1.** PRESS, compress, pinch, CRUSH, squish *squeeze into a small space* **2.** HUG, embrace *squeeze a child*

stab *(v.)* PIERCE, STICK, spear, gore, lance, hack, puncture, ENTER, penetrate, perforate

stable *(n.)* stall, barn, shed

stable *(adj.)* **1.** fixed, steadfast, solid, FIRM *a stable fence* **unstable,** FLIMSY **2.** enduring, lasting, CONSISTENT, PERMANENT *a stable government* **tentative,** TEMPORARY **3.** staunch, resolute *a stable outlook* **4.** SANE, rational *a stable personality* **irrational,** CRAZY

stage *(n.)* **1.** platform, theater, playhouse *an actor on the stage* **2.** STEP, DEGREE, point, period *a stage in a frog's development*

stage *(v.)* **1.** PLAN, ARRANGE, PRODUCE *stage a fund-raiser* **2.** PERFORM *stage a play*

stain *(n.)* smudge, MARK, smear, blemish, SPOT

stain *(v.)* soil, sully, begrime, tarnish, blot, blemish

stale *(adj.)* **1.** OLD, DRY, musty, moldy *stale bread* FRESH
2. uninteresting, trite, COMMON, flat *a stale joke*
(2) old hat

stand *(n.)* **1.** stall, booth, kiosk *a lemonade stand* **2.** dais, lectern, pulpit, rostrum *speak from a stand*

stand *(v.)* **1.** RISE, arise *Stand on a chair.* **2.** BEAR, endure, suffer, stomach, tolerate, sustain *stand the pain* RESIST

◆ **Guess the Idiom** ◆

clue: stale

answer: old hat

stare *(v.)* GAZE, gape, gawk, ogle, peek, SPY
keep an eye on
STAIR

Go **CRAZY** with **WORDS!**

stare

121

start (*n.*) **1.** beginning, threshold, verge, outset *the start of the game* ending **2.** origin, CAUSE, ROOT, SOURCE *the start of Earth Day*

start (*v.*) **1.** BEGIN, commence, initiate, launch, open, INTRODUCE *Start the music.* END, CEASE, **discontinue**, HALT, CONCLUDE **2.** originate, CAUSE, arise, rouse *start trouble* STOP **3.** startle, JUMP, flinch *start from the loud noise*
(1) hit the road, get one's feet wet, get cracking

◆ **Guess the Idiom** ◆

clue: start

answer: get one's feet wet

state (*n.*) **1.** COUNTRY, commonwealth, LAND, nation *Hawaii was the fiftieth state to join the union.* **2.** CONDITION, situation, plight *a state of confusion*

state (*v.*) TELL, EXPRESS, DECLARE, CLAIM, assert

station (*n.*) **1.** STOP, terminal, depot *a train station* **2.** PLACE, location, situation, STAGE *Each leg of the relay race began at a different station.*

statue (*n.*) monument, sculpture, casting

stay (*n.*) SUPPORT, brace, prop, buttress

stay (*v.*) **1.** WAIT, REMAIN, loiter, LINGER, dawdle, tarry, lag, PAUSE, REST, repose, abide *Stay for a few minutes.* LEAVE, **depart** **2.** STOP, CHECK, HOLD, restrain *stay the disease* **3.** DELAY, detain, hinder, HOLD *stay the decision* **continue**
(1) plant oneself, stick around

◆ **Guess the Idiom** ◆

clue: stay

answer: plant oneself

steady *(adj.)* **1.** CONSISTENT, REGULAR, CONSTANT, invariable, uniform, unfluctuating *She had a steady pulse.* **unsteady, erratic, inconsistent 2.** FIRM, fixed, STABLE, unyielding *a steady base for the marble sculpture* **unstable**

steal *(v.)* **1.** TAKE, ROB, loot, plunder, filch, thieve, fleece, poach, pilfer, despoil, purloin *steal the jewels* **2.** kidnap, abduct *steal the child*
STEEL

steep *(adj.)* SHEER, abrupt, precipitous

steer *(v.)* navigate, pilot, DIRECT, GUIDE, CONDUCT, GOVERN
be in the driver's seat

step *(n.)* **1.** STAGE, POINT, period *a step in the printing process* **2.** stair, rung, tread *He climbed each step of the ladder.*

stick *(n.)* ROD, mace, club, staff, wand, truncheon

stick *(v.)* **1.** glue, PASTE, bind *Stick the pieces together.* **2.** adhere, CLING, ATTACH *stick to a wall*

stiff *(adj.)* **1.** RIGID, unbending, inflexible, FIRM, unyielding *a stiff piece of leather* **limp, SOFT, pliant 2.** STRICT, severe, stern, austere *a stiff penalty* **lenient, lax**

still *(n.)* silence, QUIET, CALM

still *(v.)* muffle, stifle, CALM, suppress, censor, mute, quell

still *(adj.)* **1.** CALM, motionless, inactive, dormant, stagnant, STABLE, inert, stationary, tranquil, placid, serene *The boat disturbed the still water.* ACTIVE, **mobile 2.** hushed, mute, QUIET, noiseless *a still audience* NOISY, LOUD

still *(adv.)* yet, however, nevertheless

stingy *(adj.)* SELFISH, CHEAP, tightfisted, frugal, thrifty, miserly, penny-pinching, ungenerous GENEROUS, **giving**

stink *(v.)* SMELL, reek, stench

stir *(v.)* **1.** churn, WHISK, BEAT, MIX, agitate *Stir the mixture.* **2.** MOVE, BUDGE *stir from the tent* **3.** awaken, arouse, ALERT, DISTURB, stimulate, prompt *stir the dogs*

stone *(n.)* ROCK, mineral, gem, jewel, pebble

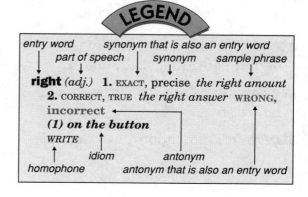

LEGEND

entry word   synonym that is also an entry word
part of speech   synonym   sample phrase

right *(adj.)* **1.** EXACT, precise *the right amount* **2.** CORRECT, TRUE *the right answer* WRONG, incorrect
(1) on the button
WRITE
homophone   idiom   antonym   antonym that is also an entry word

stop (*v.*) **1.** HESITATE, WAIT, PAUSE *Stop at the gate before you go in.* **proceed,** START **2.** HALT, END, FINISH, discontinue, stem, CEASE, QUIT, STAY, SHUT, CLOSE, CHECK, CANCEL, desist, terminate, culminate, suspend, CONCLUDE, abort *Stop the violence.* BEGIN, COMMENCE, CONTINUE **3.** prohibit, PREVENT, BAN, outlaw, FORBID, oppose, overrule *Stop the hunting.* ALLOW, PERMIT **4.** arrest, restrain, foil, CHECK, BLOCK, impede *Stop an enemy in its tracks.*
(2) cut short, call it a day, hold your horses

◆ **Guess the Idiom** ◆

clue: stop

answer: **hold your horses**

store (*n.*) shop, market, mart, depot, boutique, stall, booth

store (*v.*) SAVE, KEEP, stow, stock, hoard, reserve

storm (*n.*) downpour, hurricane, gale, tornado, cyclone, typhoon, deluge, tempest, squall

storm (*v.*) ATTACK, assault, RAID, overrun

story (*n.*) **1.** TALE, fable, novel, LEGEND, myth, fiction, romance, fantasy, parable, narrative, account *Read a story.* **2.** LIE, fib, falsehood *caught telling a story* **3.** level, FLOOR, STAGE, tier *the second story of the building*

straight (*adj.*) **1.** direct, unswerving, undeviating *a straight path* TWISTED, CROOKED **2.** FAIR, honorable, HONEST, upright *straight conduct*
(1) as the crow flies
STRAIT

strange (*adj.*) ODD, WEIRD, QUEER, CURIOUS, peculiar, UNUSUAL, atypical, UNIQUE, abnormal, uncommon, EXTRAORDINARY, quirkish **commonplace, ORDINARY**

stranger (*n.*) FOREIGNER, outsider, visitor, alien **FRIEND**

stray (*v.*) WANDER, rove, ROAM, straggle, meander

stray (*adj.*) LOST, wandering, homeless, unwanted

strength (*n.*) **1.** POWER, MIGHT, force, vigor, fortitude *the strength of the team* **weakness** **2.** sturdiness, soundness, solidity *the strength of the wood*

strengthen (*v.*) fortify, reinforce, empower **weaken, debilitate**

stress *(n.)* **1.** strain, pressure, tension, anxiety, apprehension *relief from the stress* **2.** emphasis, accent, WEIGHT, EFFORT, exertion, force *place stress on doing a good job*

stress *(v.)* emphasize, underline, accentuate

stretch *(v.)* **1.** tighten, PULL, strain *stretch a rope* CONTRACT **2.** EXTEND, lengthen, INCREASE, elongate *stretch a practice session* **3.** EXAGGERATE *stretch the truth*

strict *(adj.)* **1.** RIGID, demanding, inflexible, unbending, stringent, stern, vigilant *a strict teacher* **lenient 2.** severe, STIFF *a strict penalty* **lenient, moderate 3.** FORMAL, prim, straitlaced, CORRECT, austere *a strict dress code*

strike *(v.)* **1.** HIT, pound, PUNCH, swat, assault, ram, collide, smite *Strike the punching bag.* **2.** delete, OMIT, ELIMINATE, CANCEL *Strike from the entry list.* ADD, **include**

string *(n.)* THREAD, cord, rope, line, cable, tie

strip *(n.)* PIECE, length, slip, BAND

strip *(v.)* **1.** undress, disrobe, UNCOVER, doff *strip down to one's underwear* **2.** divest, REMOVE, deprive *strip a leader of power*

stroll *(v.)* saunter, amble, promenade, ramble
stretch your legs

strong *(adj.)* **1.** powerful, mighty, forceful, commanding *a strong coach* **2.** muscular, athletic, STURDY, SOUND, TOUGH, hardy, hale, robust, stalwart *a strong athlete* WEAK, FEEBLE, **frail 3.** potent, extreme, INTENSE *strong coffee* BLAND, **tasteless,** DILUTED **4.** ENTHUSIASTIC, ardent, zealous *a strong supporter* **indifferent, casual**

struggle *(n.)* **1.** FIGHT, QUARREL, CONTEST, conflict, skirmish *break up a struggle* **2.** LABOR, EFFORT, exertion *a struggle to survive*

struggle *(v.)* **1.** ATTEMPT, WORK, strive, LABOR, toil *struggle to meet a deadline* **2.** FIGHT, oppose *They struggled with the town council.*

stubborn *(adj.)* **1.** headstrong, willful, DETERMINED, contrary, unyielding, unbending, obstinate *a stubborn attitude* FLEXIBLE, **yielding 2.** enduring, PERSISTENT, tenacious, persevering *a stubborn illness* TEMPORARY

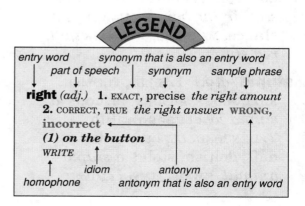

LEGEND

entry word   synonym that is also an entry word
    part of speech   synonym   sample phrase

right *(adj.)* **1.** EXACT, precise *the right amount* **2.** CORRECT, TRUE *the right answer* WRONG, **incorrect** ←
(1) on the button
WRITE

        idiom   antonym
homophone   antonym that is also an entry word

study (*n.*) **1.** den, office, studio, sanctum *Sit in the study.* **2.** examination, analysis *a study of the wetlands*

study (*v.*) READ, EXAMINE, INSPECT, INVESTIGATE, RESEARCH, scrutinize, peruse
bone up on, crack a book, hit the books

• Guess the Idiom •

clue: study

answer: hit the books

stuff (*n.*) **1.** belongings, property, assets *Let's move our stuff to the new house.* **2.** EQUIPMENT, trappings, merchandise, wares, goods, paraphernalia *all the stuff in the box* **3.** MATTER, substance, MATERIAL *What is that red stuff?*

stupid (*adj.*) **1.** SILLY, FOOLISH, RIDICULOUS, ABSURD, fatuous *a stupid joke* **reasonable** **2.** DENSE, DULL, DUMB, idiotic, daft, doltish, stolid *a stupid animal* SMART, INTELLIGENT

3. uneducated, illiterate, IGNORANT, brutish *a stupid response to the question* **educated**

sturdy (*adj.*) **1.** RUGGED, hardy, robust, stout, stalwart *a sturdy ship captain* **frail** **2.** TOUGH, FIRM, STRONG, durable *a sturdy container* FLIMSY, FRAGILE

style (*n.*) **1.** WAY, METHOD, MANNER, mode, technique, system, approach *style of living* **2.** FASHION, chic *the latest style*

subject (*n.*) **1.** theme, topic, POINT, MATTER, CONTENT, substance *the subject of the report* **2.** dependent, subordinate, INFERIOR *the king and his subjects*

substitute (*n.*) replacement, proxy, alternate, backup, standby, surrogate

substitute (*v.*) CHANGE, REPLACE, exchange, interchange, SWITCH

subtract (*v.*) REDUCE, withdraw, OMIT, ELIMINATE, REMOVE, EXCLUDE, deduct ADD, INCREASE

succeed (*v.*) **1.** ACHIEVE, accomplish, attain, prosper, flourish, thrive *succeed at school* FAIL **2.** FOLLOW, ensue *Who succeeded the last president?* **precede**

success (*n.*) **1.** achievement, accomplishment *success in a new job* **failure** **2.** FORTUNE, LUCK, welfare, prosperity *success in life* **misfortune, poverty**

sudden *(adj.)* abrupt, RAPID, surprising, unexpected, unanticipated, unforeseen GRADUAL, **deliberate**

suggest *(v.)* **1.** propose, advise, intimate *He suggested we go for a swim.* **2.** HINT, indicate *Coughing suggests a cold.*

suit *(v.)* fit, QUALIFY, SATISFY, comply

sulk *(v.)* fret, scowl, mope, glower, brood, muse

summary *(n.)* synopsis, outline, abstract, brief, digest

sunrise *(n.)* dawn, dawning, LIGHT, daybreak, MORNING SUNSET

sunset *(n.)* evening, sundown, nightfall, dusk, twilight SUNRISE

superb *(adj.)* FINE, EXCELLENT, SPLENDID, admirable, worthy, distinguished, EXTRAORDINARY, superior, striking, WONDERFUL

supply *(n.)* reserve, STORE, stock, hoard, inventory, stockpile, cache **withhold**

supply *(v.)* GIVE, PROVIDE, FURNISH, PRODUCE, bestow, confer, allocate, replenish **withhold**

support *(n.)* AID, HELP, assistance **hindrance**

support *(v.)* **1.** MAINTAIN, HELP, ASSIST, BACK, patronize, abet *support the family* **oppose** **2.** CONFIRM, reinforce, substantiate, corroborate *The evidence supports the decision.* **3.** BEAR, CARRY, uphold, BRACE, buttress, prop, STAY *support the weight* **(1) bring home the bacon**

sure *(adj.)* **1.** CERTAIN, definite, CONFIDENT, positive, proven, unfailing *a sure success* **doubtful, uncertain** **2.** CONFIDENT, decided, settled, convinced *a sure feeling about the decision* **3.** SAFE, SECURE *a sure place to hide* **unprotected, DANGEROUS, UNSAFE** **4.** dependable, reliable, FAITHFUL, tested, trustworthy *a sure friend* **untrustworthy in the bag**

surprise *(v.)* ASTONISH, AMAZE, astound, bewilder, dumbfound, THRILL, startle, awe, DAZE

surrender *(v.)* YIELD, ABANDON, renounce, relinquish HOLD, KEEP, **retain**

suspect *(v.)* **1.** distrust, mistrust, DOUBT *suspect his honesty* **2.** THINK, BELIEVE, IMAGINE, GUESS, conjecture, ASSUME, presume *suspect that something will happen* **(1) smell a rat**

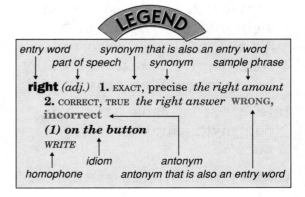

swamp (*n.*) bog, marsh, moor, morass, quagmire

swear (*v.*) **1.** CURSE, blaspheme *swear out loud* **2.** vow, affirm, assert *swear to continue*

swell (*v.*) INCREASE, ENLARGE, dilate, EXPAND, distend SHRINK, DECREASE, **contract**

swim (*v.*) wade, dip, paddle, plunge, float, glide

switch (*v.*) CHANGE, TURN, shift, replace, swap

sword (*n.*) blade, saber, cutlass, rapier, foil

symbol (*n.*) **1.** emblem, insignia, badge, totem, trademark, SIGN, token, FIGURE *The flag is a symbol of the school.* **2.** simile, metaphor, imagery *The eagle in the story is a symbol for freedom.*

Tt

take (*v.*) **1.** CHOOSE, select, PICK *Take a card from the deck.* **replace** **2.** RECEIVE, ACCEPT *take a gift from one's friend* GIVE **3.** GRAB, STEAL, ROB, seize, CAPTURE, deprive *take what does not belong to you* **free,** RETURN

tale (*n.*) STORY, fable, LEGEND, fiction, myth, parable
TAIL

talent (*n.*) GIFT, SKILL, ABILITY, aptitude, knack, expertise, dexterity, adroitness

talk (*v.*) SPEAK, SAY, TELL, chat, chatter, COMMENT, GOSSIP, lecture, DECLARE, CLAIM, prattle, converse, assert, divulge

tall (*adj.*) **1.** HIGH, lofty, elevated, towering *the tall, 20-story building* SHORT **2.** BIG, LARGE *A giraffe is a tall animal.* SMALL, TINY

tame (*adj.*) OBEDIENT, domesticated, WILLING, meek, MILD, docile, housebroken WILD, **untamed**
under one's thumb

◆ **Guess the Idiom** ◆

***clue:* tame**

answer: under one's thumb

task (*n.*) DUTY, WORK, JOB, LABOR, undertaking, chore, assignment

taste (*n.*) **1.** FLAVOR, zest *the taste of the food* **2.** JUDGMENT, discernment, liking, preference *good taste in clothes*

taste (*v.*) SAMPLE, partake, TRY, EXPERIENCE, savor, relish

Go **CRAZY** with **WORDS!**

taste

teach *(v.)* EDUCATE, TRAIN, drill, INSTRUCT, enlighten, INFORM, DIRECT LEARN, **discover**

teacher *(n.)* instructor, educator, tutor

team *(n.)* SIDE, faction, GROUP, crew, BAND, COMPANY, PARTY, GANG

tear *(n.)* HOLE, slit, rent, fissure

tear *(v.)* RIP, slash, slit, pull, SPLIT, rend **mend**

tease *(v.)* *mock,* pester, BOTHER, RIDICULE, taunt, INSULT, jeer, badger, torment, harass, provoke, vex, tantalize, gibe, deride ***drive someone nuts***

tell *(v.)* **1.** notify, INFORM, advise, recite *Tell someone about the election.* **2.** CONFESS, STATE, MENTION, proclaim, relate, ANNOUNCE, divulge, recount, disclose, reveal, profess *Tell the truth.*
(1) break the news

temper *(n.)* **1.** disposition, MOOD, humor, NATURE, CHARACTER *looking for a dog with a sweet temper* **2.** ANGER, irritation, animosity, hostility *Control your temper.*

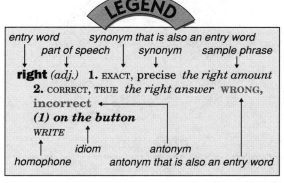

LEGEND

entry word   synonym that is also an entry word
   part of speech   synonym   sample phrase

right *(adj.)* **1.** EXACT, precise *the right amount*
2. CORRECT, TRUE *the right answer* WRONG, incorrect
(1) on the button
WRITE
   idiom   antonym
homophone   antonym that is also an entry word

129

temper *(v.)* **1.** soften, reduce, moderate *temper his anger* **2.** harden *temper steel*

temporary *(adj.)* passing, BRIEF, fleeting, short-lived, momentary, transient PERMANENT

tempt *(v.)* LURE, ATTRACT, seduce, LEAD, PERSUADE, entice, induce

tender *(adj.)* **1.** SOFT, DELICATE, FRAGILE *tender skin* **2.** compassionate, KIND, GENTLE, loving *tender loving care* **HARSH, unkind, MEAN 3.** SENSITIVE, painful *a tender wound*

tense *(adj.)* **1.** uneasy, ANXIOUS, worried, concerned, stressed, apprehensive *a tense person* **relaxed, CALM 2.** TIGHT, stretched, strained, RIGID, taut *a tense rope*
(1) all wound up
TENTS

terrible *(adj.)* HORRIBLE, AWFUL, frightful, dreadful, GHASTLY, HORRID, dire, hideous, grisly WONDERFUL, MARVELOUS, **terrific**

test *(n.)* QUIZ, examination, trial

test *(v.)* EXAMINE, evaluate, QUESTION, TRY
bounce something off someone

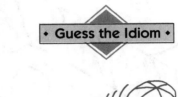

• **Guess the Idiom** •

clue: test

answer: bounce something off someone

thankful *(adj.)* GRATEFUL, obliged, indebted, beholden **ungrateful**

therefore *(adv.)* consequently, accordingly, thus, then

thick *(adj.)* **1.** WIDE, DEEP, bulky, solid, squat, stodgy *thick stone walls* **THIN, NARROW, SKINNY 2.** gooey, gummy, DENSE, viscous *a thick liquid* **runny, watery**

thief *(n.)* ROBBER, bandit, brigand, pirate, plunderer, burglar, swindler, pickpocket, looter

• **Guess the Idiom** •

clue: tense

answer: all wound up

thin *(adj.)* **1.** SLIM, SKINNY, LEAN, spare, slender, underweight, drawn, lank *a thin person* FAT **2.** NARROW *thin ice* WIDE **3.** SHEER, FINE, diaphanous *thin fabric* THICK

thing *(n.)* **1.** OBJECT, ITEM, entity, contraption, article, DEVICE, GADGET *Pack your things.* **2.** act, deed, EVENT *Peculiar things have happened.*

think *(v.)* **1.** ponder, WONDER, meditate, REFLECT, CONSIDER, contemplate, IMAGINE, envisage, ruminate *Think about recycling.* **2.** BELIEVE, suppose, IMAGINE, presume, ASSUME, conceive, suppose, surmise *He thinks we should pay lower taxes.* **3.** STUDY, EXAMINE, JUDGE, deliberate *Think about the clues.*
(3) use your head

thought *(n.)* IDEA, notion, fancy, reflection, CONCEPT, perception, impression, supposition

thoughtful *(adj.)* **1.** CONSIDERATE, KIND, attentive *thoughtful enough to send flowers* inconsiderate, RUDE **2.** reflective, pensive, studious, wistful, nostalgic *thoughtful about the past* **3.** mindful, prudent, heedful *always thoughtful of others* IGNORANT, **rash**

thoughtless *(adj.)* CARELESS, inconsiderate, neglectful, heedless, negligent CAREFUL, CONSIDERATE

thread *(n.)* fiber, cord, filament

threaten *(v.)* **1.** menace, intimidate, torment, terrorize *Threaten the dog.* **2.** loom, impend, forebode *A storm threatens to engulf the town.*

thrill *(v.)* PLEASE, EXCITE, arouse, stimulate
tickled pink

throw *(v.)* toss, sling, FLING, hurl, PITCH, CAST, chuck, pelt, project, shoot, PASS

tickle *(v.)* **1.** TOUCH, stroke, titillate *tickle one on the arm* **2.** PLEASE, AMUSE, DELIGHT *She was tickled by the gift.*

tie *(n.)* necktie, cravat

tie *(v.)* **1.** knot, snag *Tie a bow.* **2.** fasten, hitch, JOIN, ATTACH, link, fetter, hobble *Tie the boat to the dock.* **3.** WRAP, bind, bundle, secure, truss *Tie up the package.*

tidy *(adj.)* CLEAN, NEAT, orderly, organized, IMMACULATE MESSY, SLOPPY, **disheveled**

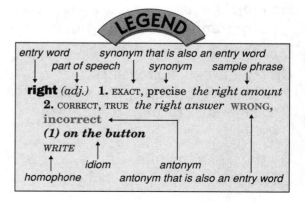

LEGEND

entry word — synonym that is also an entry word
part of speech — synonym — sample phrase

right *(adj.)* **1.** EXACT, precise *the right amount* **2.** CORRECT, TRUE *the right answer* WRONG, **incorrect** ←
(1) on the button
WRITE

homophone — idiom — antonym — antonym that is also an entry word

tight *(adj.)* **1.** close-fitting, taut, FIRM, SECURE, clingy *a tight diving suit* LOOSE **2.** STINGY, close-fisted *a tight budget* GENEROUS, **giving**

time *(n.)* period, term, interval, PAUSE, gap, season, SPELL, age, interlude
THYME

timid *(adj.)* SHY, bashful, modest, retiring, reserved, demure
afraid of one's own shadow

• Guess the Idiom •

clue: timid

answer: afraid of one's own shadow

tiny *(adj.)* LITTLE, SMALL, wee, puny, miniature, dwarf HUGE, **massive**, LARGE, IMMENSE

tip *(n.)* **1.** END, POINT, PEAK, extremity *the tip of the pencil* **2.** REWARD, gratuity *a tip for the waiter*

tip *(v.)* LEAN, incline, tilt

tired *(adj.)* sleepy, drowsy, WEARY, fatigued, sluggish, jaded **rested, invigorated, refreshed**

together *(adv.)* joint, UNITED, concerted ALONE, SEPARATE

tool *(n.)* GADGET, appliance, utensil, contraption, DEVICE, INSTRUMENT, apparatus, implement

top *(n.)* **1.** lid, COVER, stopper, cap *the top of the jar* **2.** apex, acme, pinnacle, zenith *the top of her class* BOTTOM **3.** PEAK, crest, summit, TIP, crown *the top of the mountain* BASE

total *(n.)* SUM, TOTAL, WHOLE, AMOUNT, QUANTITY **portion**, PART

total *(adj.)* COMPLETE, FULL, ENTIRE **partial, incomplete**

touch *(v.)* FEEL, HANDLE, grope, finger, fondle, EXPERIENCE

tough *(adj.)* **1.** STRONG, FIRM, RUGGED, hardy, stalwart *a tough acrobat* TENDER, **delicate** **2.** lasting, durable *made of tough plastic*

toy *(n.)* trinket, plaything

toy *(v.)* trifle, PLAY, dally, jest, dabble

trade *(v.)* swap, EXCHANGE, barter

train *(v.)* EDUCATE, INSTRUCT, TEACH, tutor, school, drill, COACH, discipline

traitor *(n.)* renegade, deserter, rebel, turncoat, dissident, heretic

Go CRAZY with WORDS!

touch

translate (v.) EXPLAIN, interpret, decode, clarify, SOLVE, unravel, decipher **code, encode**

transport (v.) CARRY, BEAR, haul, DELIVER, CONVEY

trap (v.) CATCH, GRAB, CAPTURE, seize, arrest, snare, ensnare, entrap RELEASE, FREE
bait the hook

trash (n.) rubbish, GARBAGE, WASTE, JUNK, REFUSE

travel (v.) MOVE, journey, ramble, VOYAGE, PASS, traverse

treat (v.) **1.** USE, HANDLE, wield, MANAGE *Treat the tools with care.* **2.** ENTERTAIN, AMUSE, CHEER *treat my friends to a great show* **3.** nurse, doctor, minister, remedy *Treat the wound.* **4.** finance, spend, fund *Treat the children to pizza.*

trick (n.) **1.** JOKE, gag, hoax, fraud, jest, antic, prank, caper, ILLUSION, deception, delusion *He played a trick on his friend.* **2.** LURE, wile, stratagem *They used a trick to catch the thief.*

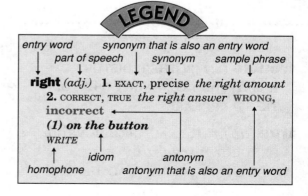

LEGEND

entry word   synonym that is also an entry word
    part of speech   synonym   sample phrase

right (adj.) **1.** EXACT, precise *the right amount*
2. CORRECT, TRUE *the right answer* WRONG,
incorrect
(1) on the button
WRITE
    idiom   antonym
homophone   antonym that is also an entry word

133

trick (*v.*) FOOL, bluff, DECEIVE, outwit, CHEAT, delude, dupe, defraud
pull the wool over one's eyes

trip (*n.*) JOURNEY, outing, VOYAGE, flight, expedition, passage, VISIT, tour, excursion, pilgrimage

trip (*v.*) FALL, stumble, falter, flounder, stagger

troop (*n.*) troop, COMPANY, squad *TROUPE*

trouble (*n.*) **1.** difficulty, hardship, inconvenience, toil *car trouble* **2.** DISTRESS, suffering, adversity *He made trouble in the family.*
(2) a real pickle

◆ Guess the Idiom ◆

clue: trouble

....

answer: a real pickle

---

trouble (*v.*) BOTHER, DISTURB, inconvenience, ANNOY, vex, DISTRESS APPEASE

true (*adj.*) **1.** REAL, actual, valid, GENUINE *a true ruby* FAKE, **phony 2.** CORRECT, ACCURATE, confirmable *a true statement* FALSE, **untrue, bogus**
3. HONEST, upright, FAITHFUL, sincere, GENUINE, LOYAL, steadfast, SOUND, reliable, dependable, trustworthy *a true love* **unfaithful**

trust (*n.*) FAITH, CONFIDENCE, belief, reliance, assurance **distrust, suspicion**

trust (*v.*) BELIEVE, DEPEND, rely ***count on***

truth (*n.*) FACT, reality, certainty, actuality, veracity, verity, verisimilitude LIE, **falsehood**

try (*v.*) **1.** ATTEMPT, SEEK, STRUGGLE, AIM, strive, aspire, endeavor, venture *Try to reach the top of the mountain.* **2.** SAMPLE, TASTE, EXPERIENCE *Try eating an oyster.*
3. undertake, tackle *Try scuba diving.*
(1) bend over backward

◆ Guess the Idiom ◆

clue: try

....

answer: bend over backward

tumble (v.) FALL, stumble, topple

tune (n.) jingle, SONG, melody

turn (n.) CHANCE, period, stint, shift, stretch

turn (v.) **1.** SPIN, revolve, rotate, screw *Turn the knob.* **2.** REVERSE, swivel, hinge, BEND, TWIST, pivot, invert *Turn around.* **3.** CURVE, swerve, maneuver, jockey, veer *Turn to the left.* **4.** DIVERT, AIM, DIRECT, point *He turned his attention away from the problem.*

twist (v.) **1.** wring *Twist the towel.* **2.** writhe, contort *twist and turn while dancing* **3.** wind, encircle *Twist the cord around the bag.*

type (n.) KIND, SORT, CLASS, GROUP

Uu

• •

ugly (adj.) unattractive, unsightly, homely, GHASTLY, hideous **PRETTY, HANDSOME, GORGEOUS**

uncover (v.) disclose, reveal, EXPOSE, divulge, BARE, unwrap, DISCOVER **COVER, CONCEAL**

understand (v.) COMPREHEND, SEE, GET, DRAW, grasp, perceive, CONCLUDE, deduce, fathom, resolve *get the picture, get it through your head, put two and two together*

unfriendly (adj.) aloof, distant, COLD, HOSTILE, malevolent **FRIENDLY, cordial, WARM, hospitable**

unhappy (adj.) SAD, cheerless, GLOOMY, BLUE, sorrowful, tragic, downcast, dispirited, depressed, pessimistic, morose, crestfallen, despondent, doleful, woeful, mournful, melancholy, wretched, hapless, forlorn **HAPPY, GLAD, joyous, cheerful, spirited, gleeful, jubilant**

unique (adj.) RARE, UNUSUAL, exceptional, distinctive, SPECIAL, matchless **COMMON, USUAL**

unimportant (adj.) petty, slight, paltry, trivial, trifling, insignificant **IMPORTANT, significant *nothing to sneeze at***

united (adj.) **1.** joined, TOGETHER, combined *the United States* **SEPARATE, INDEPENDENT** **2.** agreeing, harmonious, unanimous *united in their opinions* **divided, combative, contentious**

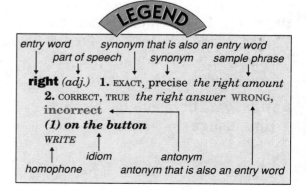

135

unnecessary *(adj.)* NEEDLESS, USELESS, dispensable, expendable, irrelevant, superfluous NECESSARY, ESSENTIAL

untrue *(adj.)* **1.** FALSE, WRONG, incorrect, INACCURATE, erroneous *an untrue statement* TRUE, CORRECT **2.** unfaithful, disloyal, treasonous, traitorous, deceitful, dishonorable *an untrue friend* FAITHFUL, **dependable, reliable**

unusual *(adj.)* UNIQUE, DIFFERENT, STRANGE, ODD, CURIOUS, uncommon, unconventional, unprecedented, exceptional USUAL, **commonplace**, ORDINARY, **standard, everyday**

unwilling *(adj.)* opposed, averse, loathe, reluctant, disinclined WILLING, **compliant**, READY

upset *(v.)* **1.** BOTHER, DISTURB, perturb, ANNOY, IRRITATE, rattle, OFFEND, disgust, outrage, disconcert *upset one's mother* **appease, pacify 2.** overturn, capsize, invert *upset the canoe* **3.** BEAT, OVERTHROW *upset the competition*
(1) make waves, tie in knots

urge *(v.)* **1.** BEG, plead, beseech *urge one to continue* **2.** PUSH, PRESS, DRIVE, FORCE, impel *The jockey urged his horse on.*

use *(n.)* utility, benefit, application, usage

use *(v.)* **1.** utilize, apply, EMPLOY, avail, wield, HANDLE, brandish *use all my skills to do the job* **2.** expend, consume, EXHAUST *use up the gas*

useful *(adj.)* **1.** HELPFUL, HANDY, practical, efficient, beneficial *a useful tool* USELESS **2.** SOUND, QUALIFIED, serviceable, applicable *a useful suggestion*

useless *(adj.)* **1.** pointless, valueless, worthless *a useless vehicle* USEFUL, NECESSARY, **practical 2.** fruitless, futile, vain, frivolous *a useless attempt* **beneficial, effective**

• **Guess the Idiom** •

clue: upset

answer: tie in knots

usual *(adj.)* NORMAL, COMMON, REGULAR, FAMILIAR, customary, FREQUENT, habitual UNUSUAL, **irregular, uncommon**

Vv

vague (*adj.*) uncertain, doubtful, obscure, indefinite CLEAR, OBVIOUS, **specific, distinct**
on the fence

clue: vague

answer: on the fence

valiant (*adj.*) BRAVE, DARING, courageous, intrepid, GALLANT, heroic, valorous, chivalrous COWARDLY, **fearful**

valley (*n.*) glen, ravine, gorge, gulch, crater, chasm, abyss, vale

valuable (*adj.*) **1.** PRECIOUS, costly, priceless, EXPENSIVE *a valuable piece of jewelry* **worthless**
2. IMPORTANT, USEFUL, HELPFUL, beneficial *a valuable lesson*

value (*n.*) **1.** WORTH, importance, merit, stature *the value of a* good education **2.** PRICE, COST, fare, RATE *The value of baseball cards has increased.*

vanish (*v.*) DISAPPEAR, DISSOLVE, FADE, evaporate APPEAR, **materialize**
go down the drain

clue: vanish

answer: go down the drain

variety (*n.*) **1.** KIND, TYPE, SORT, CLASS *a rare variety of day lily* **2.** assortment, diversity *a variety of colors*

vary (*v.*) CHANGE, alter, deviate, differ CONTINUE

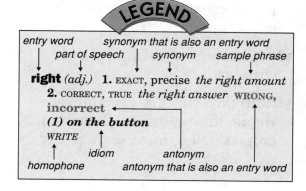

LEGEND

entry word   synonym that is also an entry word
part of speech   synonym   sample phrase

right (*adj.*) **1.** EXACT, precise *the right amount*
2. CORRECT, TRUE *the right answer* WRONG, **incorrect**
(1) on the button
WRITE
homophone   idiom   antonym   antonym that is also an entry word

vast *(adj.)* HUGE, ENORMOUS, IMMENSE, colossal **cramped, minute**

vehicle *(n.)* carriage, carrier, conveyance, transport

verbal *(adj.)* oral, spoken, stated, unwritten, told **non-verbal**

verdict *(n.)* JUDGMENT, decision, finding, OPINION, sentence

vertical *(adj.)* upright, plumb, erect, perpendicular HORIZONTAL

vessel *(n.)* **1.** container, receptacle *a clay vessel* **2.** ship, boat, craft *a sailing vessel*

vibrate *(v.)* SHAKE, QUAKE, tremble, quiver, oscillate, twitch

vicious *(adj.)* WICKED, CRUEL, ruthless, BRUTAL, SAVAGE KIND, **docile, gentle, virtuous**

victim *(n.)* PREY, loser, scapegoat, sufferer, quarry **assailant**

victory *(n.)* triumph, conquest, SUCCESS, mastery DEFEAT

view *(n.)* **1.** SCENE, vista, survey, sight, vision, spectacle *a beautiful ocean view* **2.** OPINION, JUDGMENT, belief, hunch, impression, perspective *one's view on after-school sports*

view *(v.)* survey, scan, behold, WITNESS

villain *(n.)* CRIMINAL, scoundrel, rogue, knave, outlaw, hoodlum, culprit, felon, miscreant HERO

violent *(adj.)* raging, WILD, unruly, riotous, disorderly, FURIOUS, turbulent, wrathful **peaceful,** GENTLE, MILD

visit *(v.)* **1.** CALL, STOP, sojourn *visit a neighbor* **2.** TALK, chat, converse *visit on the phone*

voice *(n.)* articulation, words, tone, SPEECH, utterance, LANGUAGE

voyage *(n.)* JOURNEY, TRIP, expedition, cruise

Ww

wages *(n.)* salary, PAY, earnings, compensation

wage *(v.)* **1.** undertake, CONDUCT, pursue *wage war against an enemy* **2.** BET, stake, GAMBLE *wage a dollar*

wait *(v.)* **1.** STAY, PAUSE, REMAIN, LINGER, lag, dawdle *Wait a moment.* CONTINUE, **proceed, resume 2.** HESITATE, waver, tarry, loiter, DELAY, postpone, falter *He waited to make the decision.*
(1) hold your horses, keep your shirt on
WEIGHT

wake *(v.)* rouse, arouse, awaken, stimulate, STIR SLEEP

Go CRAZY with WORDS!

walk

WALK

STROLL

JOG

RUN

RACE

walk (*v.*) STEP, hike, STROLL, trek, stride, trudge, shuffle, tramp, tread, MARCH, tiptoe, amble, saunter, promenade **jog,** RUN, RACE

wall (*n.*) barricade, fence, obstacle

wander (*v.*) **1.** ramble, rove, range, ROAM, STRAY *The cows wander over the field.* **2.** swerve, deviate *The car wandered all over the road.*

want (*v.*) HOPE, DESIRE, hunger, crave, yearn, WISH, LONG, hanker, REQUIRE, aspire

war (*n.*) conflict, battle, COMBAT, warfare PEACE

warm (*adj.*) **1.** tepid, heated, sunny *warm water* COOL, CHILLY **2.** cordial, FRIENDLY, open, welcoming *a warm welcome* RUDE, **brusque, distant**

warn (*v.*) **1.** ALERT, CAUTION *warn the villagers* **2.** INFORM, notify, advise, admonish, CRITICIZE *warn someone not to do it again*

wash (*v.*) cleanse, SCRUB, launder, swab

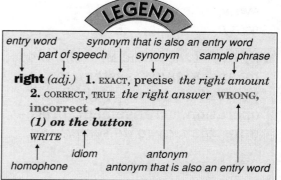

LEGEND

entry word   synonym that is also an entry word
   part of speech   synonym   sample phrase

right (*adj.*) **1.** EXACT, precise *the right amount* **2.** CORRECT, TRUE *the right answer* WRONG, incorrect
   (1) on the button
   WRITE

homophone   idiom   antonym
            antonym that is also an entry word

waste (n.) **1.** GARBAGE, TRASH, REFUSE, rubbish *dispose of waste* **2.** excrement, sewage *human waste* **3.** loss, misuse *a waste of time*
WAIST

waste (v.) **1.** dwindle, wither, perish, pine, wane *slowly waste away* **2.** fritter, squander, SCRAP, lavish, dissipate *waste money* SAVE **3.** dally, trifle, dawdle *waste time doing nothing*
WAIST

watch (v.) MIND, ATTEND, OBSERVE, regard, spectate, behold, VIEW, WITNESS

water (n.) **1.** river, stream, brook, creek, rivulet, brook, bourn, spring, fountain, ocean, sea, billows *Throw the pebble in the water.* **2.** tide, current, ebb, flow, torrent *The water came up to the sand dunes.*

water (v.) irrigate, moisten, sprinkle, dampen

wave (n.) ripple, swell, breaker, billow, surge, undulation
WAIVE

wave (v.) flutter, flap, swing, sway, VIBRATE
WAIVE

way (n.) **1.** MANNER, METHOD, mode, means, FASHION, system, STYLE, process, structure, technique, operation, arrangement, procedure *the way to do something*

2. COURSE, PATH, ROUTE, track *on the way to school*
WEIGH

weak (adj.) **1.** frail, FRAGILE, FLIMSY, unsound, DELICATE *a weak chair* STURDY, STRONG, **potent** **2.** FEEBLE, infirm, sickly, debilitated, sluggish, decrepit, languid *a weak child* HEALTHY, STRONG **3.** powerless *a weak army* **invincible, forceful** **4.** thin, watery, diluted, impotent *weak tea* STRONG **5.** DIM *a weak light* **bright**
(2) on your last legs
WEEK

wealth (n.) riches, treasure, FORTUNE, abundance, affluence **poverty**

wear (v.) **1.** clothe, invest, don *Wear your new belt.* **2.** IRRITATE, fray *wear on one's nerves* **3.** PRODUCE, CREATE *wear a hole in a rug*
WARE

weary (adj.) TIRED, fatigued, exhausted, sleepy, drowsy, sluggish, jaded **rested, ALERT**

weave (v.) plait, braid, interlace

weep (v.) CRY, sob, lament, wail, whimper, blubber, mourn

weight (n.) **1.** heaviness, burden, LOAD, gravity *the weight of the logs* **2.** importance, import, INFLUENCE, SCOPE *the weight of public opinion*
WAIT

weird *(adj.)* **1.** ODD, STRANGE, UNUSUAL, CURIOUS, UNIQUE, peculiar *a weird sound* **natural** **2.** QUEER, mysterious, bizarre, eerie, uncanny *a weird set of circumstances* ORDINARY, COMMON

welcome *(n.)* greetings, salutation, reception

welcome *(v.)* GREET, receive, salute, hail, host

well *(n.)* spring, fountain, SOURCE

well *(adv.)* **1.** HEALTHY, sound, hearty, hale *feeling well* **2.** satisfactorily, correctly *do well on the test*
(2) with flying colors

◆ **Guess the Idiom** ◆

clue: well

···
answer: with flying colors

wet *(adj.)* **1.** DAMP, moist, soggy, soaked, saturated, drenched, flooded *a wet towel* DRY, parched, brittle **2.** rainy, humid *a wet day* DRY, **arid**

wharf *(n.)* PIER, jetty, landing, quay

whine *(v.)* CRY, whimper, moan, groan, grumble, snivel
WINE

whip *(v.)* lash, scourge, PUNISH, BEAT, flog

whole *(adj.)* COMPLETE, undivided, ENTIRE, intact, unbroken, SOUND **partial**, INCOMPLETE, PART
HOLE

wicked *(adj.)* BAD, EVIL, unprincipled, IMMORAL, VICIOUS, sinful, sinister, CORRUPT, villainous, unscrupulous, depraved KIND, GOOD, **virtuous**

wide *(adj.)* LARGE, BROAD, VAST, extensive, roomy, spacious NARROW, THIN

wild *(adj.)* **1.** untamed, SAVAGE, barbarous, uncivilized *a wild animal* **2.** FEROCIOUS, raving, frenzied, HYSTERICAL, VIOLENT, delirious, turbulent *a wild attack*

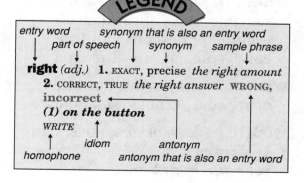

LEGEND

entry word   synonym that is also an entry word
   part of speech   synonym   sample phrase

right *(adj.)* **1.** EXACT, precise *the right amount* **2.** CORRECT, TRUE *the right answer* WRONG, incorrect ◄—
(1) on the button
WRITE

homophone   idiom   antonym
antonym that is also an entry word

willing (*adj.*) READY, agreeable, inclined, disposed UNWILLING, averse

win (*v.*) **1.** SUCCEED, triumph, BEAT, overcome, OVERTHROW, vanquish *win at tennis* LOSE, **forfeit** **2.** ACQUIRE, EARN, GAIN, procure *win a prize* LOSE, **squander** **(1) take the cake**

◆ **Guess the Idiom** ◆

clue: win

answer: take the cake

wipe (*v.*) RUB, polish, CLEAN, swab, mop

wisdom (*n.*) SENSE, sensibility, intelligence, insight

wise (*adj.*) INTELLIGENT, learned, sensible, sage, shrewd, acute, erudite, philosophical **ignorant**, FOOLISH, **uneducated**

wish (*n.*) will, DESIRE, intention, GOAL, HOPE, REQUEST, mandate

wish (*v.*) WANT, DESIRE, HOPE, hanker, crave *set your heart on*

witness (*n.*) spectator, bystander, onlooker

witness (*v.*) **1.** SEE, behold, OBSERVE, WATCH, NOTE *witness a crime* **2.** attest, testify *witness before a judge*

witty (*adj.*) FUNNY, amusing, SHARP, droll

wizard (*n.*) **1.** magician, sorcerer, conjurer *The wizard concocted a magic potion.* **2.** EXPERT, authority, master, whiz, virtuoso *She was a wizard with computers.*

wonder (*n.*) awe, amazement, astonishment

wonder (*v.*) THINK, ponder, meditate, speculate, peruse, marvel

wonderful (*adj.*) MARVELOUS, SPLENDID, INCREDIBLE, amazing, astonishing, miraculous, stupendous, EXTRAORDINARY, spectacular TERRIBLE, AWFUL, HORRIBLE

◆ **Guess the Idiom** ◆

clue: wish

answer: set your heart on

wood *(n.)* timber, log, lumber, plank, BOARD
WOULD

woods *(n.)* forest, woodland, grove, thicket, bush

word *(n.)* **1.** term, phrase, label *Spell the word.* **2.** statement, report *a word from our sponsor* **3.** PROMISE, pledge *Keep your word.*

work *(n.)* **1.** JOB, employment, profession, calling, DUTY, function *the work of a teacher* **play, sport, recreation** **2.** EFFORT, drudge, drudgery, grind, exertion, travail *a lot of work* **3.** RESULT, EFFECT *good work*

work *(v.)* **1.** toil, LABOR, grind, function, exert *work at the office* PLAY, **frolic, dally** **2.** OPERATE, HANDLE, CONDUCT, manipulate, MANAGE *work the machine* **3.** function, PERFORM *The radio does not work.* **4.** SHAPE, FORM *work the clay*

workers *(n.)* employees, crew, staff, faculty, personnel, labor, laborers

worn *(adj.)* SHABBY, faded, RAGGED, threadbare, SORRY

worry *(n.)* CONCERN, CARE, anxiety, DISTRESS, agitation

worry *(v.)* **1.** fret, CARE, FUSS, fidget, grieve *worry about one's grades* **2.** BOTHER, DISTURB *worry your parents* **3.** TEASE, pester, harass, torment, tantalize, harry, plague *worry the dog*
(1) be tied up in knots

worship *(v.)* ADORE, RESPECT, idolize, venerate, revere

worth *(n.)* **1.** VALUE, COST, valuation, appraisal, assessment, evaluation, CHARGE, expense *the worth of a house* **2.** merit, QUALITY, virtue, integrity *the worth of a person*

wound *(n.)* CUT, injury, ulcer, laceration, abrasion, trauma

wrap *(v.)* ENCLOSE, envelop, surround, encircle, COVER, muffle, bundle, truss, shroud, enshroud **unwrap, OPEN, reveal, uncover**
RAP

wreck *(v.)* DESTROY, RUIN, RAZE, demolish, sack, annihilate, decimate

wrinkle *(n.)* crease, furrow, pucker

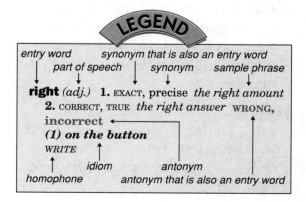

write (*v.*) **1.** jot, SCRIBBLE, scrawl, pen, PRINT, NOTE, imprint, inscribe, engrave *Write your name on the paper.* **2.** COMPOSE, author, draft *write a story* **3.** document, RECORD *Write down the results of the experiment.* **4.** correspond, COMMUNICATE, ANSWER *Write your grandparents soon.* RIGHT

wrong (*adj.*) **1.** FALSE, UNTRUE, incorrect, mistaken, INACCURATE, erroneous *the wrong answer* CORRECT, RIGHT **2.** BAD, WICKED, IMMORAL, IMPROPER, unjust, CORRUPT *on the wrong side of the law* JUST, GOOD **(1) out in left field**

Yy

yard (*n.*) grounds, garden, court, enclosure, compound

yell (*v.*) SHOUT, CALL, SCREAM, screech, shriek

yield (*n.*) **1.** crop, harvest, PRODUCT *a good yield of corn* **2.** REWARD, recompense, interest *the annual yield on your savings account*

yield (*v.*) **1.** BEAR, PRODUCE, impart, confer *yield a good harvest* **2.** SURRENDER, relent, submit, defer, relinquish, succumb *yield to the enemy*

young (*n.*) CHILDREN, offspring, litter, brood

young (*adj.*) youthful, childish, immature, infantile, juvenile, junior, puerile OLD, senior, adult **wet behind the ears**

youth (*n.*) **1.** child, youngster, MINOR, dependent, juvenile *an after-school recreation program for youths* adult **2.** adolescence, childhood *in one's youth* adulthood, maturity

Zz

zany (*adj.*) FOOLISH, SILLY, wacky, goofy, nonsensical **sensible, logical**

zeal (*n.*) ENTHUSIASM, passion, fervor, ardor

zero (*n.*) nothing, none, nil, naught, null

zone (*n.*) REGION, AREA, district, quarter, territory, locality, tract